A BOOK OF

Spinning Wheels

A BOOK OF
Spinning Wheels

by *Joan Whittaker Cummer*

Photographs by
Bob La Pree
and
Rosamond G. Shaw

PETER E. RANDALL PUBLISHER
PORTSMOUTH · 1993

Peter E. Randall Publisher
Box 4726, Portsmouth, NH 03802

ISBN 0-914339-46-x

Foreword

Spinning wheel collectors, antique dealers, and those curious about their family heirlooms will find the photographs and text in this volume very helpful. Joan Whittaker Cummer has provided us with excellent photographs, careful measurements, and judicious comments about each wheel. Studying these photographs is a thrill for anyone interested in textile tools and knowing that the wheels themselves will be available for study at the Museum of American Textile History (MATH) in Lowell, Massachusetts, is especially exciting. Readers will be able to identify what they have and learn something of it.

Over the almost twenty-five years I have been collecting and studying spinning wheels I have encountered many collections and collectors. S. D. Stevens and his family provided the original collection and impetus for what became MATH. Mr. Stevens in the United States and John Horner in Ireland were aggressive collectors at the turn of the century. The latter's collection is at the Ulster Museum and line drawings from it are widely published. Marion Channing of Marion, Massachusetts, had a small but interesting collection in addition to her excellent work as a textile tool historian in the 1960s. Anne Pixley of Duxbury, Massachusetts, whose large collection also ended up at MATH, was another eager self-taught student of spinning wheel history. William Leinbach of Myerstown, Pennsylvania, has a superb collection of wheels and a deep interest in their history. Dave Pennington, Jim Munsie, and I have all been avid collectors of wheels and their history since 1969 although Dave has by far the largest and most interesting collection of the three. All of these people have been extremely helpful to others in the process of building their collections. They have willingly and even passionately shared their knowledge and enthusiasm for spinning wheels, and these are but the tip of the iceberg as I have encountered many other collectors here and there over the years and in no way mean to slight them or their collections. Visiting with such afflicted people is a real joy. Only a fellow sufferer can appreciate why with thirty-some wheels already and no place for them, you couldn't live without a fifteen-foot long patent wheel!

Often after such a visit with a new friend or an old one, I wish I had taken a better photograph or another measurement or had asked another question. Occasionally, I am gratified as I look at the pictures I took and the notes I made, but usually I want more. After visiting with Joan Cummer and her collections I always wanted more than I had taken away because there was so much there. In this book there are 130 wheels pictured—and such wonderful wheels! Finally, I can really appreciate the breadth and depth of the collection. To see it in person was to be overwhelmed. There was never enough time. Now we can all enjoy it and linger over a wheel for however much time it takes to appreciate it.

Of course, looking at the collection was only part of the joy of the visit because Joan is such a resource as she patiently answers questions about her wheels. She is always more careful in her answers and skeptical, but respectful, of the anecdotal information that often accompanied a purchase. She patiently endures even my most off-the-wall speculations to this day and over the years I have had some odd ones. In the text accompanying the photographs, Joan's judicious and informed comments are an important contribution and worth weighing carefully.

One of the things I am learning from Joan is a greater appreciation for European wheels. I tend to focus and value only "American" wheels even though I am aware that a very small percentage of antique wheels are American in design. My favorite wheel has always been the Irish Castle wheel which I think of as an American because it was made by a number of makers in the Lancaster, Pennsylvania, region, but that is pretty silly as the version I am particularly fond of is the one that is virtually identical to those found in the Ulster region of Ireland. It is of such bias and nonsense that Joan has almost weaned me over the years.

Beyond overcoming such ethnocentrisms, Joan's book helps collectors see some of the roots of American wheels. Immigrants off the boat clearly made wheels very similar if not identical to the ones they knew and made "back home." It was only over time and through contact with others that a European design evolved into an Americanized version. So a thorough study of European wheels is an important part of one's "spinning wheel education."

Of course, in some cases American ingenuity or sheer cussedness did come up with something radically different, and this book has some wonderful examples of that. Some of these examples are of types fairly well-known, such as the Connecticut chair wheel, but others are very rare and to my knowledge one is unique (the bobbin and flyer wheel in an enclosed cabinet). Her example of the original patented version of Lyman White's "pendulum wheel" is also very important for collectors to see as very few were made in that fashion. I am sure every reader will see several they have never before encountered or even imagined. Every reader will see some they wish they had. More than a few lucky ones will recognize one they have and learn something about it.

Spinning wheel collectors often end up collecting other related textile tools and Joan is no exception. So there is a chapter on the fascinating artifacts that are associated and sometimes confused with spinning wheels.

I am delighted that Joan has made her collection and knowledge available in this wonderful book and through the Museum of Textile History. She has made an important contribution.

Dr. Michael Taylor
Marietta College

Contents

Acknowledgments

Having decided to write a book about spinning wheels it became quickly apparent this was not a one-woman enterprise.

First there must be a photographer to take pictures. My life long friend, Rosamond Grenfell Shaw from Wayne, Pennsylvania volunteered. Under her expertise I learned the complications of background, angles, and lighting. She devoted days and made a great contribution to the work before returning to Pennsylvania. Then Mr. Bob La Pree of Contoocook, New Hampshire, accepted the assignment of editing the existing pictures and photographing the rest of the collection of wheels and accessory tools. Most of this work was done in November in the unheated building where the wheels were stored. Without the good will, kindness, and expertise of these two people this book would never have existed.

I would also like to thank Ellen Heston of Hillsborough, New Hampshire, who spent freezing cold days placing the wheels one by one, and adjusting them an inch this way, and inch that, so that Bob could get them at the best angle. Her patience and perseverance were greatly appreciated.

Another heroine was "friend Bea," Mrs. Beatrice Achorn of Lyndeborough, New Hampshire, who so kindly spent long days with me recording the multiple measurements of each wheel so that the tables of comparative measurements could be made.

And finally I would like to thank my friend Trudi Toll who initiated me into the bewildering world of book publishing, and without whose help this book could never have seen the light of day.

Preface

The spinning wheels pictured in the following pages belong to the Cummer collection of wheels and related artifacts, now in possession of the Museum of American Textile History in Lowell, Massachusetts. They illustrate the types and styles of spinning equipment from the beginning of the eighteenth century to 1948. They have almost all been purchased in New England over the last thirty-five years. Some were made in New England and in other parts of the United States. Some came to New England with immigrants from Europe and Canada. Some, especially over the last ten years, have been imported from Europe by antique dealers. No two wheels are alike; each has its own special characteristic.

It is difficult to say with exact surety where a wheel originated. However, certain types of wheels seem to have been most popular in certain areas of Europe. For instance, vertical wheels with thick wheels and uprights are found in Poland, north east Germany and the Ukraine, while vertical wheels, of much lighter construction, with the treadle to the side instead of under the wheel, are found in Switzerland and south west Germany. However a wheel maker in the new world might make a wheel similar to those he remembered in his own country, or he might reproduce a wheel his neighbor had brought from Europe. Under each picture is stated the country from which the wheel is thought to have come. Unless the place of origin is known for a fact the word "probably" precedes the place.

Just as the actual place of origin is difficult to ascertain so is the age of the wheel. One expert will look at a wheel and say "Eighteenth century." A month later another expert will declare the same wheel to be "Definitely nineteenth century," while a third expert will announce it could be either. The age of each wheel, therefore, has been stated as "probably," and the figure that follows has been arrived at as a consensus of opinion. For the few wheels where the age is definitely known it is so stated.

At the end of the book, tables of measurements are presented. These measurements are helpful when comparing wheels or identifying a wheel not in the book. The ratio of the wheel diameter to the whorl diameter is a guide to the speed that particular wheel can deliver the twist to the thread. Other factors, however, chiefly workmanship, also affect the speed. The number of spokes and legs are also recorded because this is the question most often asked by someone trying to identify a wheel.

This book is offered as a tribute to the individuality of the men who made the wheels and to the spinners who used them.

The Spinning Wheel Collection

O ften I have been asked what prompted me to collect spinning wheels. Like most of the good things we do, it was not a conscious, premeditated decision; it just happened. Some people rescue dogs, some little birds fallen from nests; I rescued spinning wheels.

It all began one spring day when I was captivated by a pair of Dorset lambs and carried them home to my children. But lambs (as I had forgotten) grow into sheep, and sheep must be shorn when the days become longer and warmer. Back in 1950 very few people had ever seen a sheep sheared. So I found a shearer, invited the school children to come for the morning, and sat back to watch the event. When the shearing was finished I had two large piles of dirty, greasy fleece which I contemplated with curiosity and repugnance. I looked at the white sweater I was wearing —it was wool. I looked at the dirty piles—they were wool. Suddenly I was filled with determination to change those piles into sweaters.

In the 1950s there were no handspinners at fairs and craft shows and no "how to" books on spinning published. Being completely ignorant, I decided the first thing I needed was a spinning wheel. At that time all the antique stores had a selection of spinning wheels and twenty-five dollars would buy any wheel in the country. So home I came with what is now known as "the great Canadian," or Quebec wheel. I read the *Encyclopedia Britannica* (1930 ed.), bought a pair of carders from the Timothy Eaton mail order catalogue (Sears did not carry them), and launched myself into production. Production ended with about six yards of lumpy, greasy string. The wheel went into the attic, the fleece to the dump, and I to other matters. Ten years later spinning began to revive. I found a young woman to teach me, discovered I had a wheel better suited to an expert than a beginner, and was once again enthralled with turning fleece into spun yarn. At this time, a second wheel came to live with me, a much slower, gentler old Quebec wheel.

One day, while waiting for a friend, I listened to a New York lady and a New Hampshire antique dealer bargaining over a beautiful, small, obviously usable wheel. To my horror I realized from their conversation she was going to cut a hole in the wheel table, put in a potted ivy, and turn that fine little wheel into a decoration for a New York apartment. One could not let that happen, and so wheel number three came to live with me. Four and five soon followed; one was a double flyer wheel, the other a Connecticut chair wheel. Then odd ones drifted in, little irresistible parlor wheels, a Shaker wheel, and some pretty strange ones. My children were overheard telling someone, "If you want to sell Ma a wheel, just tell her it will make a good planter. She'll go for it every time." And, in truth, when I bought one of my last wheels, the multiple spinner (wheel no. 21) the dealer actually told me it would make a good planter or a frame for displaying quilts.

In the years preceding the renaissance of hand spinning many wheels were destroyed or desecrated. People have told me that when they emptied "Grandma's" old house for resale, they dug a pit, put all that old "junk" from the attic in it, and had a great bonfire. Antique dealers painted old wheels white or pink or flamingo orange, nailed them to their porch roofs or mounted them on a pole and they became their sign: "The White Lady Antiques" or the "Pink Wheel Shop."

I live in a small house and the wheels were stashed away in corners, under the staircase and in the guest room. By the time I had about twenty-two wheels, I noticed the house guests were becoming awkward and grumpy. I think the collection might have stopped there had it not been for a miracle. In Webster, New Hampshire, stands the Old Webster Meeting House built in 1798. It is cared for and looked after by "The Friends of the Old Webster Meeting House." The first floor is filled with treasures from Webster's past. The second story was empty. Two of the Friends were also members of the New Hampshire Spinners and Dyers Guild and thanks to their kind offices I was invited to put the wheels on display in the second story. It is due to the generosity of the The Friends of the Old Webster Meeting House that the collection grew to its final size.

Wheels came from unexpected places and in unexpected ways. Sometimes someone would call to tell me of a strange wheel she had seen, or someone who wanted to sell a wheel would contact me. Flea markets, auctions, antique shows sometimes produced a treasure or two. When Mr. McNeil, an antique dealer from California with a devotion to spinning wheels, moved to Antrim, New Hampshire, things really happened. We have had a joyous association for the last ten years.

But wheels like everything else require care. Subjected to the temperature changes of an unheated building, they had to be oiled to prevent drying and cracking. This meant long hot hours every summer going over each wheel with linseed oil and turpentine. Eventually it became necessary that some decision about the collection's future must be made. When the Museum of American Textile History offered the wheels a home in their permanent collection it was obviously the right solution. It was hard to see them go (rather like when your youngest child left for college), but it was a good and appropriate place for these wheels. I look back with joy on the years I had them and hope that other people will enjoy them in the years to come.

IDENTIFICATION OF WHEEL PARTS

1. distaff
2. distaff holder
3. maidens
4. mother-of-all
5. flyer
6. bobbin
7. whorl
8. tensioner
9. table
10. wheel posts
11. treadle
12. footman
13. treadle
14. spindle post
15. spindle
16. accelerating head

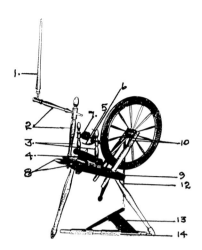

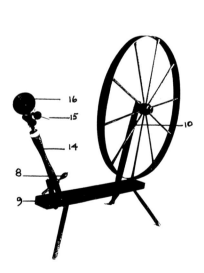

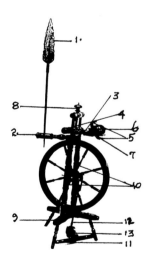

A Brief History of
Spinning Wheel Development

The art of spinning has its roots in the earliest dawn of civilization, for, until a continuous thread was fashioned, no clothing other than from skins or grass could be made. The spinning wheel, however, is a relatively modern invention. Before the fourteenth century all spinning was done by using either a drop or a supported spindle. In many parts of the world today this is still the preferred method of hand spinning. Spindles are easily made, very portable and uncumbersome.

The first spinning wheels came to Europe from India and their use spread along the trade routes. These had a simple straightforward mechanism. A wheel, turned by hand, was connected by a driving band to a spindle. The greater the ratio of the diameter of the wheel to the diameter of the driving band groove on the spindle, the faster the spindle turned as the wheel revolved.

The very early wheels appear to have been small, about two feet long with three or four inch legs. The spinner sat on the ground or on a low stool to work. In Europe, possibly because the ground was colder and wetter, these evolved into the great "walking wheels" so named because the spinner stood to spin and stepped backwards, sideways and forward as she worked. Whether sitting or standing the spinner turned the wheel with one hand, drew out the fibres from the tip of the turning spindle with the other, thus giving them the twist. When the thread extended to arms length, the spinner brought it in from the tip to the back of the spindle, then, turning the wheel as she stepped forward, she wound it onto the body of the spindle. A rhythm was established of drawing out the fibres, allowing them to twist, then winding them on the spindle.

The next advance in spinning wheel design was the development of the flyer-bobbin assembly to replace the spindle. This allowed the drawing out of the fibres and the winding on of the thread to be accomplished simultaneously. The first wheels of this type seem to have appeared in Italy and Germany about the late fifteenth century. These wheels at first were turned by one hand while the spinner's other hand drew out the fibres. Their advantage was speed and efficiency in spinning long flax fibres and long wool staples. Also the spinner could now sit comfortably to work. The treadle seems to have been added in the early seventeenth century, possibly in the Netherlands or England.

The efficacy of the bobbin-flyer wheels depends on the bobbin and the flyer turning at different speeds. The usual way to accomplish this is for the bobbin and the flyer whorls to be of different diameters and each driven by the same common double driving band. Since both are being driven by the same rotating wheel, this creates a differential in the turning rates of the bobbin and the flyer, and so the thread is drawn on to the bobbin. Another method is to use a single drive band and to have another band pass over the flyer near the orifice, which can be tightened as needed. This is called a flyer-brake tension. Or, just as well, the bobbin may be slowed by a band passing over the bobbin, over a bar across the tops of the maidens, then fastened to the mother-of-all by an adjustable screw. This method is often referred to as a "Scottish Tension" because of its popularity in Scotland. Indeed there it is often used in conjunction with the double drive band. It is felt to give the spinner greater control facilitating the spinning of a softer yarn.

As the bobbin fills with thread it is essential that tension on the driving band be increased in order to maintain the drawing in speed. In wheels using a single double drive band this is accomplished most commonly by a large wooden threaded screw passing into the front end of the table and through the bulbous block on which is mounted the mother-of-all (see diagrams on page 4). The block fits into an aperture cut in the front table top. As the screw handle is turned the block moves, bringing the mother-of-all nearer or farther from the wheel, decreasing or increasing the tension on the band, and thus decreasing or increasing the turning speed of the bobbin.

In the nineteenth century, in Canada, a "rocker tensioning" method was developed. Here the mother-of-all is cradled on the table and held in place by a large U bolt or a heavy metal clamp. By loosening a thumbscrew on the U bolt or clamp, the mother-of-all may be sloped towards or away from the wheel, then tightened into the desired position. Occasionally variations on this method are found. On one wheel the mother-of-all is attached to a metal plate which slides into the grooves of another metal plate fastened to the front end of the table. By loosening a thumb screw the mother-of-all's plate can be slid closer or further from the wheel thus changing the tension on the band.

For vertical wheels there are two types of common tensioning devices (See page 4). One has a bar that joins the tops of the uprights that support the wheel and carry the mother-of-all. A tensioning screw passes through this bar and into the mother-of-all which can be raised or lowered as the screw is turned. The other type has a chock fitted into a slot in the back upright, and this supports the bobbin-flyer assembly. A tensioning screw passes through the top of the upright into the chock which can then be raised or lowered, lifting or dropping the bobbin-flyer assembly as required.

In the sixteenth and seventeenth century spinning wheels flourished all over Europe and the British Isles. Orphans and women in the poorhouses and prisons were taught to spin on the wheel as a means of making a livelihood. "Spinning Factories" existed. These consisted of warehouses equipped with the tools for hand carding and combing the fleece and many spinning wheels. The wages paid the spinners were a pitiful pittance. By the late seventeenth century double flyer wheels, with which the spinner spun with both hands at once, were in use. Using such a wheel, a spinner, though unable to double her production, could greatly increase her hourly output. It is interesting that in the United States only, these wheels were duped "gossip wheels."

Towards the end of the eighteenth and in the nineteenth centuries small wheels were fashionable among the upper class women. It also became a custom for young women to have a "trousseau" wheel when they married. These wheels were beautifully turned and often decorated with inlay, marquetry, pewter, pearl, bone, and ivory. There were also small wheels gaily painted in bright colors. These little wheels were neither for children, nor toys, nor peddlars' samples. They were used in drawing rooms. The wear visible on the treadles and orifices, and the quality of the thread often found remaining on the old bobbins bear silent witness to the diligence and skill of the ladies who used them.

An improvement in the spindle wheels appeared at the beginning of the nineteenth century when Amos Minor, living in New York state, patented an accelerating head which greatly increased the turning speed of the simple spindle. This head consisted of a small wheel, approximately four inches in diameter, mounted directly over the drive groove on the spindle. The driving band of the great wheel passed over the hub of this wheel. Another driving band went around the small wheel's rim and around the groove of the spindle thereby in essence creating a gear. This head was so successful in increasing the speed of the walking wheel it was manufactured by a number of companies and widely used in America. Old wheels on which the original "bat heads" have been replaced by an accelerating head are commonly found today. The use of an accelerating wheel was soon adopted by some bobbin-flyer wheel makers, notably the wheel known as the Connecticut chair wheel. Later in the nineteenth century wheels employing an accelerating wheel were made in the province of Quebec.

The last half of the nineteenth century found a burgeoning of radical new shapes and designs of American spinning wheels. The great pendulum wheel of L. Wight was patented in 1857. In 1871 Hathorn patented a complicated spinner-cum-winder. In 1872 Bryce patented a metal table model. In 1878, in Canada, T. H. Nute of Nova Scotia patented a wooden "spinning, reeling and quilling machine" that clamped to a table. The above wheels were all of the spindle type. However during the same period variations in bobbin-flyer wheels using accelerating mechanisms appeared. These variations do not seem to have enjoyed as large a popularity as the patented spindle wheels.

In the early twentieth century spinning wheel production was at a low ebb, although as late as 1940 the mail order catalogue of the T. Eaton Co., of Canada still sold them. During the twenties and thirties wheels were still being made in the Canadian provinces of Quebec and Manitoba. During the 1960s, possibly as a reaction against mass production, more leisure time and the need for self expression, there occurred a revival of interest in hand spinning. Old wheels were brought out of storage, oiled, refurbished and put to use. New wheels, largely from New Zealand were imported to America. By 1975 new wheels, usually reproducing the classic designs of the earlier centuries, were being made in the United States, Canada, Europe, England, Australia, and New Zealand. In British Columbia very large bobbin-flyer assemblies with big orifices were being mounted on cabinets of old treadle sewing machines. These were used by the Salish Indians spinning bulky yarn for their famous Cowichan sweaters. Later the electric sewing machine replaced the old treadle sewing machine to drive the bobbin flyer. In Samarkand, U.S.S.R., in 1987, a young woman was observed spinning cotton on a spindle driven by an electric motor. Although electricity is providing the power to turn the spindle or the bobbin-flyer assembly the fibres are still drawn out and guided by the hand spinner. Finally in the 1980s new, completely redesigned, electric spinners were made by several companies for the hand spinners. Truly hand spinning has kept pace with civilization.

CLASSIFICATION OF WHEELS

The naming of different types of wheels depends largely on local customs. For instance, the common large wheel that drives a spindle may be called a wool wheel, a walking wheel, a great wheel or, in Scotland, a muckle wheel. The bobbin-flyer wheels are often referred to as flax wheels, saxony wheels, parlor wheels or even spinning wheels (as opposed to the "wool wheel"). In the Shetland Islands an upright bobbin-flyer wheel is called a "spinney" while a horizontal bobbin-flyer wheel is a "wheel" or "the wheelie". In this volume the wheels are classified as follows.

SPINDLE WHEELS:
These are those wheels which directly turn a spindle by a connecting driving band.

BOBBIN-FLYER WHEELS:
These are those wheels where the fibres are twisted by the turning flyer and simultaneously drawn on to the bobbin. Usually these wheels are treadled and the wheel drives the bobbin-flyer assembly by means of a single double drive band. The greatest variety of wheels is found in this category, so they have been subdivided into:

(a) *Horizontal Wheels:* These have a table at one end of which is mounted the wheel (referred to as the back end), and at the other end the bobbin-flyer assembly (referred to as the front end.).

(b) *Vertical wheels:* These usually have very small round or rectangular tables over which is the wheel. Above the wheel and sometimes a few inches to one side is the bobbin-flyer assembly.

(c) *Parlor wheels:* These wheels are the very small wheels, averaging approximately eleven inches in diameter, with tables about fifteen inches long for the horizontal wheels. Some are vertical wheels. Most of them have elaborate turnings and many have ivory bone, pewter or inlay decoration.

(d) *Double Flyer wheels:* These are wheels that carry two flyers on one wheel and treadle, allowing a spinner to spin with both hands at once.

(e) *Castle wheel:* The castle wheels are vertical wheels with the wheel at the top and the bobbin-flyer assembly well below it. (The Irish castle wheel is the only one in the collection.)

Spindle Wheels

WHEEL NO. I

This wheel, thought to have been made in Europe in the very early 18th or possible late 17th century, is the oldest in the collection. It came to the United States in a shipment of antiques from Portugal to Mr. Bob McNeil of Antrim, New Hampshire. This does not mean it necessarily originated in Portugal, but certainly somewhere in western Europe. Patricia Baines book, *Spinning Wheels, Spinners and Spinning,* on page 57, shows an engraving of a spinning room using such wheels. It must have been unbelievably back breaking work.

The spindle is missing on this wheel. The wheel supports are primitive. One seems to have been eaten by rats, rot or mold. There are worm holes throughout. The long sides of the table are beaded. The two posts which held the spindle are artistically shaped at the top and attractively chip carved, around the edges.

HEIGHT: 52.5 in.
DEPTH: 16 in.
LENGTH: 105.5 in.

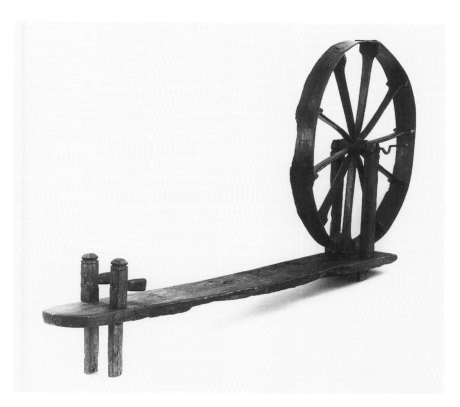

WHEEL NO. I

WHEEL NO. 2

This wheel probably comes from India or Indo China. It is impossible to estimate its age, but it is thought to be neither modern nor of great antiquity, probably nineteenth century. Its chief point of interest is that this design is unchanged from the earliest spinning wheels known.

The wheel is rimless. A lacing passes back and forth from spoke to spoke. The drive band rests on this lacing and passes to the multi-grooved spindle. In spite of being made from hard wood, (probably teak) the frame has elaborate carving. On the cross piece under the wheel appear fishes or eels, and in the center a face. The design on the long board, the wheel supports and small areas is geometric, suggestive of flowers and trees. There is a hole in the handle large enough to comfortably insert a finger. It is unknown whether there was once a knob in this hole to hold, or whether the spinner simply inserted a finger. The leathers which hold the spindle have obviously been replaced recently. Supposedly the old ones were worn out either by use, or age, or both.

HEIGHT: 22 in.
DEPTH: 24 in.
LENGTH: 31 in.

WHEEL NO. 2

WHEEL NO. 2 DETAIL

SPINDLE WHEELS / 15

WHEEL NO. 3

This wheel, of unknown age, is from Asia Minor. Although the workmanship is delicate, the design follows the most primitive wheels.

This is a table model spindle spinning wheel, thought to have been used for spinning silk. The remains of a clamp on the bar to the right of the mother-of-all can be seen.

The whole apparatus is made of metal, which appears to be a copper amalgam. The handle on the wheel axle is wood. The edges of the "table" and all of the bar which held the clamp are decorated with turquoise hammered into the metal. The rimless wheel is comprised of two discs of hammered turquoise edged by onion shaped metal protrusions, placed half an inch apart. These discs are joined by a fine plied wire woven around the protrusion of one disc then crossing over to the protrusion of the other. The driving band is supported on this crossing wire. (See wheel no. 2).

HEIGHT: 5 in.
DEPTH: 5.5 in.
LENGTH: 12 in.

WHEEL NO. 3

WHEEL NO. 4

This wheel, known as the Charka or Ghandi wheel, was developed in the present form by Mahatma Ghandi during the late 1920s. It was designed for portability, simplicity and economy. Ghandi, hoping to free the Indians from the necessity of buying cotton from England, set an example to his followers by spinning and weaving cloth for his own clothing. Ghandi also contended everyone should spin for an hour first thing each morning for the beneficial meditative state thereby produced. This particular wheel was purchased on a street in Bombay, and bears the official British Government registration stamp.

The case holds three spindles, two used for spinning and the third for plying; also the reel for skeining. The spinner sits on the ground, on the rod which hooks over the edge of the box in order to stabilize it. After filling the third spindle with plied thread, the smaller wheel is removed and replaced by the block of wood into which the skeining arms are inserted. When the spinner is through, the skeiner, spindles, wheels and stabilizing rod fit into their appointed places, and the whole case closes. At a glance it appears to be an ordinary book 6.5 by 10 in.

A slightly larger model was also made which resembled an attaché case when closed.

HEIGHT:	1.25 in
DEPTH:	6.5 in.
LENGTH:	19.5 in. when open; 10.25 in. closed

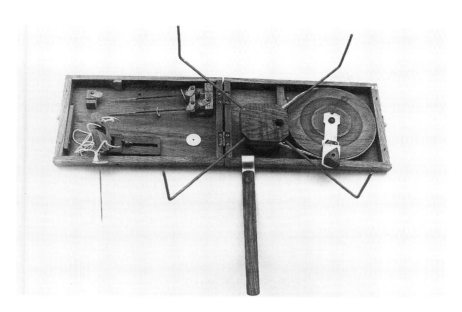

WHEEL NO. 4 IN SKEINING MODE

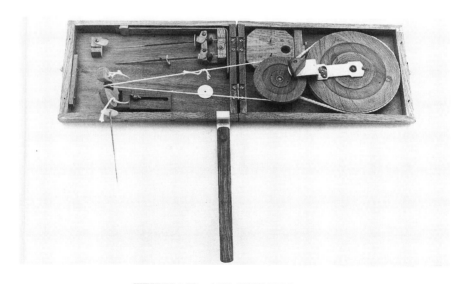

WHEEL NO. 4 IN SPINNING MODE

WHEEL NO. 5

This American spindle wheel was probably made in New England or Ohio in the early eighteenth century. Five and a half feet tall with a wheel diameter of four feet, it is exceptionally large. The spokes, posts and tensioning device are similar to the Shaker wheels. The collar on the spindle post is missing. The table has chip carving at both ends and beading along the edges. The wheel is signed "Whitelaw."

HEIGHT: 66.5 in.
DEPTH: 22 in.
LENGTH: 75 in.

WHEEL NO. 5

WHEEL NO. 6

This American spindle wheel came from the Ozark mountain region and was probably made in the latter half of the nineteenth century.

The wheel rim is only one inch wide and has flattened with age between the spokes. It has a single groove. The unusual feature of this wheel is the very steep slope of the table. The spindle tip is 52 inches from the ground. Also the spindle has a turned wooden cover for the spindle tip when the wheel is not in use. The combination of the height of the spindle tip and the cover suggests an effort was being made to protect the eyes of a young child.

HEIGHT: 58 in.
DEPTH: 21 in.
LENGTH: 60 in.

WHEEL NO. 6

WHEEL NO. 7

This wheel bears the stamp of "Benjamin Pierce," a well known wheel maker of Chester, New Hampshire, in the early nineteenth century. The table is slim and elegant with no chip carving nor beading along the edges.

The spindle post is attractively turned but the wheel post and legs are plain. All parts appear to be original. The wheel rim has three grooves for the drive band. The wheel axle is metal.

HEIGHT: 57.5 in.
DEPTH: 22 in.
LENGTH: 71 in.

WHEEL NO. 7

WHEEL NO. 8

This Shaker wheel is signed "F.W." Francis Winkley was the head elder at the Canterbury, New Hampshire, Shaker community during the early 1800's. In the case of Shaker wheels the initials do not mean that the wheel was made by that individual. The letters are the initials of the head elder at the time when the wheel was made. They are similar to an inspection sticker, showing the wheel met the high standard of production and could be marketed by the community.

This wheel is a typical Shaker design. Everything about it is plain, simple and functional. A bone collar reinforces the spindle post. Occasionally a pewter collar was used. These wheels are found quite commonly in New Hampshire today and still work smoothly and satisfactorily.

HEIGHT: 59.75 in.
DEPTH: 20.75 in.
LENGTH: 69 in.

WHEEL NO. 8

WHEEL NO. 9

This wheel, signed "D.M.," was made in the New Lebanon, New Hampshire, Shaker community, in either the very late seventeenth or early eighteenth century. The initials are believed to be those of David Meacham, the first head elder of New Lebanon.

Devoid of turnings and decorations, it is a typical Shaker wheel except for the unusual tensioning mechanism. This consists of the customary large wood screw which can be tightened against the spindle pole. But in addition there are two supports mounted into the table, one each side of spindle post, through which passes another wooden screw. This screw can be tightened by the wooden bolt which faces the spinner. The advantage of these supports is not clear. It is not a design that was adopted by other Shaker communities.

HEIGHT:	59 in.
DEPTH:	19 in.
LENGTH:	74 in.

WHEEL NO. 9

WHEEL NO. 10

This diminutive spindle wheel was undoubtedly made for a child, which makes it a very rare wheel. Children usually started spinning at six or seven years of age on the family wheels. It came to New Hampshire from the Appalachian area.

Reed or bamboo rims are attached to each side of the wheel rim to prevent the driving band from slipping off; a most frustrating experience as any spinner knows. The spindle's point has been cut off, probably as a safety measure after it was retired. It would have been eye height for a small child.

The wheel has the aura of having been made with a great deal of love.

HEIGHT: 29 in.
DEPTH: 7.25 in.
LENGTH: 21.75 in.

WHEEL NO. 10

WHEEL NO. II

This is a very simple small spindle wheel, American in origin, probably made in the early or mid nineteenth century.

There is no tensioning device. The only turnings are simple ones on the wheel posts and the spindle posts. There is chip carving along the ends of the table. The wheel is turned by a wooden handle on one of the spokes.

HEIGHT: 48.75 in.
DEPTH: 14.5 in.
LENGTH: 50 in.

WHEEL NO. II

WHEEL NO. 12

This is an early nineteenth or late eighteenth century American wheel.

The table is well made with deep chip carving at each end and two deep rows of beading along each side. The legs are chamfered. The spokes and posts are plain. The wheel is mounted by a wooden spindle to the wheel post.

The unusual feature is the tensioning device. The spindle supporting post ends in a large oval disc which passes through a slit in the table and pivots on a wooden peg that goes through the sides of the table and the disc. A large wooden screw penetrates the table and, when tightened, presses against the disc, securing it in the chosen position.

HEIGHT: 59 in.
DEPTH: 21.5 in.
LENGTH: 52.5 in.

WHEEL NO. 12

WHEEL NO. 13

Thought to have been made in the United States probably during the early nineteenth century, this wheel is most remarkably heavy and has old original red paint. The iron tensioning rod is adjusted by the decorative iron thumbscrew. The posts and spokes are without any turnings or decoration. The edges of the table are beveled. The lower half of the legs are chamfered.

HEIGHT: 61.25 in.
DEPTH: 15.5 in.
LENGTH: 51 in.

WHEEL NO. 13

WHEEL NO. 14

This wheel appears to be from the eighteenth or early nineteenth century and was probably made in New England. It is signed "A. Ballou." The wheel post is very gracefully sculptured and the wheel is mounted on it by a wooden axle. The wheel rim is constructed with two pieces which is unusual. Dual spindle posts support a block of wood between them into which is fitted an accelerating head. The block is pivoted and its position can be secured by tightening the wooden peg protruding from the back post.

HEIGHT: 55.5 in.
DEPTH: 20 in.
LENGTH: 68 in.

WHEEL NO. 14

WHEEL NO. 15

This nineteenth century wheel is thought to have been made in New England. The manner of mounting the accelerating head is similar to wheel no. 14.

Two 17.5 in. posts are mounted through the table end. Between them a barrel is supported by a .75 in. threaded dowel which penetrates the front post and passes through the back post. There it is secured by a nut. A classic Minor head is mounted through the center of the barrel. The tension of the drive band from the wheel to the Minor head is regulated by tilting the barrel back and forth and securing its position by tightening the nut.

On the table, nine and a half inches from the end, are two pleasantly-shaped pegs, three and a half inches high. It is believed that these were to keep rolags within easy reach of the spinner.

The turning on the legs, spokes, and posts are simple, restrained and well executed.

HEIGHT: 61 in.
DEPTH: 21.5 in.
LENGTH: 68 in.

WHEEL NO. 15

WHEEL NO. 16

This American spindle wheel is thought to have been made in the very late nineteenth or even early twentieth century. There are no turnings on the spokes, legs or posts except for the shaped top of the wheel post. There is some inferior chip carving along the ends of the table.

Its interesting feature is its attempt to construct a different type of accelerating action. On top of the spindle post is a block of wood on which are mounted two brass supports that hold the spindle with its 1 in. diameter whorl. Two thirds of the way down, a block of wood is fitted into the post. On this block brass supports hold a metal double wheel, one side of which has a 2 in. diameter and the other a 1 in. diameter. A single drive band passes from the large wooden wheel to the lower 1 in. diameter metal wheel. Another drive belt passes from the 2 in. side of this metal wheel up to the 1 in. whorl of the spindle. The idea is ingenious. No tensioning device exists on this wheel.

HEIGHT: 57.25 in.
DEPTH: 15 in.
LENGTH: 53.25 in.

WHEEL NO. 16

WHEEL NO. 17

This is a New England spindle wheel probably from the early nineteenth century.

The wheel is mounted to the post on a wooden spindle. The table has chip carving along the front edge.

Its interesting feature is the tensioning mechanism. The spindle post is inserted through the table and connected to the table by a wooden dowel on which it pivots back and forth. Into the post has been placed a fan shaped piece of wood with many perforations. By pushing a small peg into the appropriate perforation the desired position of the post is secured.

HEIGHT: 58 in.
DEPTH: 21 in.
LENGTH: 69.5 in.

WHEEL NO. 17

WHEEL NO. 18

This is a nicely made wheel, again thought to have come from the early nineteenth century.

This wheel also has an unusual tensioning device. There are two posts, one in front and one behind of the spindle posts. Between each post and the spindle post is a 3 inch wooden nut. By tightening or loosening these nuts the position of the spindle post is secured. Another peculiar feature of this wheel is the 3/8th-inch hole through the spindle post, 34.5 inches from the ground. Possibly this was made to accommodate a lower spindle for a child to use.

HEIGHT: 58.5 in.
DEPTH: 22 in.
LENGTH: 68 in.

WHEEL NO. 18

WHEEL NO. 19

This American wheel, probably from the early nineteenth century, is of interest because of its simple but different tensioning mechanism. The spindle post sits over a slot in the table and a large wooden thumb screw passes up through this slot into the spindle post. When the screw is loosened the post can be moved along the table and then secured in the desired place by tightening the screw.

The legs and posts have elaborate, chunky turnings. The spokes are plain with a chamfered enlargement at the rim end. The table has beading along the edges but no chip carving. The spill between the two back legs is unusual.

HEIGHT: 60.75
DEPTH: 20 in.
LENGTH: 67 in.

WHEEL NO. 19

WHEEL NO. 20

This wheel is thought to come from New England and was probably made in the mid-nineteenth century. It has a "sliding table" tensioning device. The spindle post is mounted on a piece of wood 4.5 inches wide and 18 inches long. At the post end this piece of wood is 2 inches thick, then it is cut away to 1 inch thickness. There is a slot one-inch wide and 9.5 inches long in this thin end. From under the table a large wooden screw passes through the table and through the slot described. The piece of wood can be slid backward or forward on this screw, and its position secured by tightening the large wooden bolt on the screw. The axle of the wheel where it penetrates the wheel post is a half-inch square. A rectangular piece of metal, secured to the wheel post by square, hand-made nails protects the post.

The wheel rim is a single piece. The spokes are fastened to it by pieces of bent metal like heavy staples. The legs and spindle post have one simple turning which is repeated on the more elaborately turned wheel post.

HEIGHT: 61 in.
DEPTH: 18.5 in.
LENGTH: 73 in.

WHEEL NO. 20

WHEEL NO. 21

This is a multiple spindle wheel known as a "Vertical Spinning Machine." The one photographed here is painted with old blue paint and bears the stamp "Ebenezer Ware Jr. 1831. No. 1.. It is believed to have been made in Hancock, New Hampshire. Originally it had 12 spindles; two have been lost. Also missing is the frame which fitted into the runners on the front legs.

Half the spindles were attached to the left hand whorl by a single drive belt; the other half were similarly attached to the right hand whorl. A belt went from the left whorl to the right hand whorl, which in turn had a belt going to the hand turned wheel. A metal thumb screw under each whorl allowed each to be adjusted for tension and alignment. Pencil roving was passed from piles on the floor, through the missing frame, and up to each spindle. The spinner turned the wheel with one hand while drawing the frame down, thus drawing out the fibres. The wire brackets raised and lowered the lead weights which facilitated the winding of the spun yarn onto the spindles.

HEIGHT: 69 in.
DEPTH: 27.5 in.
WIDTH: 51 in.

WHEEL NO. 21

WHEEL NO. 22

This pendulum wheel was patented by L. Wight in 1856. The spindle is mounted at the end of a five and a half foot rod which is attached to a horizontal accelerating head. The wheel is turned by hand. As with conventional spindle wheels, the speed with which it is turned controls the amount of twist given the drawn out fibres, or the speed with which the thread is wound onto the spindle. When the treadle is depressed it sends the rod holding the spindle away from the spinner thereby making the draw. The wooden ball, filled with lead, acts as a counter weight and sends the spindle back to the spinner as she lets up on the treadle. As the spindle travels back the spun thread is wound on to the spindle.

The advantage of this wheel was that, because of the prolonged draw, it increased the speed of production. Also the spinner remained sitting at her work and so, supposedly, could spin for a longer period. Wheels of this type flourished during the American Civil War and subsequent years when the supply of relatively cheap spun wool from England was cut off.

HEIGHT: 77 in. (pendulum at rest)
DEPTH: 28 in.
LENGTH: 73.25 in. (pendulum at rest)

WHEEL NO. 22

WHEEL NO. 23

This American patent wheel from the nineteenth century appears to be a stripped down, "economy" model of the L. Wight pendulum wheel (wheel no. 21).

On this wheel the counter weight ball is not encased in wood, nor is the supporting structure as massive and handsome. The wheel is mounted on the end of a 31 in. rod which is equipped with a six inch slit at the other end. This rod is mounted on to the two cross beams by two large wooden screw pegs passing through the slit. By sliding this rod and securing its position with the two wooden screw pegs the tension of the driving band is adjusted.

HEIGHT: 72 in.
DEPTH: 30.75 in.
LENGTH: 72 in.

WHEEL NO. 23

WHEEL NO. 24

The "Haythorn" wheel was patented in 1870 and they were manufactured in Maine. They have a peculiar "Rube Goldberg" quality to them.

The drive band passes around the large wheel, over the small wheel on the side of the upright post, over to the accelerating head, back around the small wheel on top of the upright post, then finally back to the large wheel. The board on which all is mounted is equipped with innumerable holes which would accommodate the Miner's head. Supposedly these were available for adjusting the tension on the drive band.

The overall effect is a sense of awe and bewilderment.

HEIGHT:	10 in. (without skeiner)
DEPTH:	21 in.
LENGTH:	16 in.

WHEEL NO. 24

WHEEL NO. 25

This spindle wheel, made in Michigan, was patented in 1872 by J. Bryce. The name "J. Bryce" is embossed on the rim of the metal wheel.

An ordinary "C" clamp fastens the machine to any table or work bench for use. The spinner may stand or sit to spin.

The machine is made entirely of metal except for the whorl on the spindle and the small solid wheel into which it fits. A rough surfaced washer on the axle insures friction necessary for turning the spindle. The pressure of the iron wheel on the small wheel axle is controlled by a thumb screw.

HEIGHT: 10 in.
DEPTH: 7.5 in.
LENGTH: 19.5 in.

WHEEL NO. 25

WHEEL NO. 26

This wheel from Nova Scotia, often referred to as the "Hurdy Wheel," was patented in 1870 by John Henry Nute. Judging from the number seen in antique shops of Canada and New England is was very popular in its time.

Mounted on a board is a driving wheel at one end, an accelerating head about one-third of the way along, and a reel complete with a counting mechanism at the other end. The whole apparatus is clamped to a bench or a table.

The driving wheel, always painted dark red with a black curved block design, can be placed on either side of the metal axle. Another Hurdy wheel in the collection actually has two wheels, one on each side of the board. Since several with two wheels have been seen it seems likely that some were produced this way. According to Buxton-Keenlyside's excellent description in *Selected Canadian Spinning Wheels in Perspective*, the wheel was placed on one side for spinning and plying and on the other side for quilling.

In New England this wheel was popular for plying heavy yarns.

WHEEL NO. 26

WHEEL NO. 27

This crude wheel may have been a quiller, a spinner or used for plying string. The wheel is solid and heavy. The spindle is wooden and whittled to a taper. It is held in place by a shaped block of wood screwed to its counter part mounted to the table. There is a large, 1.25 in. diameter, hole in the table with an adjoining indentation. Its function is not known.

HEIGHT: 14.7 in.
DEPTH: 13.5 in.
LENGTH: 23 in.

WHEEL NO. 27

WHEEL NO. 28

This wheel was originally a late eighteenth or early nineteenth American Quiller. It has been converted to a spindle wheel by attaching an accelerating head to the edge of the quiller box. This would allow a spinner to remain sitting while working. One wonders whether a grandmother, whose legs had worn out, once again felt useful and a contributing member of the family, thanks to this conversion.

HEIGHT: 38.5 in.
DEPTH: 16 in.
LENGTH: 42 in.

WHEEL NO. 28

European Horizontal Bobbin-Flyer Wheels

WHEEL NO. 29

This early eighteenth century wheel is believed to have been brought to New England from England. On the underside of the table is carved the date, 1707, in Roman Numerals. This would be compatible with the William and Mary turnings.

There is one hole in the table to accommodate a distaff. Long ago it received a coat of dark green paint which has mostly worn off showing an older finished wood under it. The dark green paint does not appear to be twentieth century. The wheel support braces come from the legs. The treadle is nailed to the treadle bar. The wheel shows a great deal of wear.

HEIGHT:	34.5 in.
DEPTH:	19 in.
LENGTH:	36 in.

WHEEL NO. 29

WHEEL NO. 30

This wheel was made in the late eighteenth or early nineteenth century in Ireland.

The turnings are Sheraton period with extremely fine reed turnings on the distaff. The third piece of the distaff is missing. The flyer on this wheel was made from a single piece of wood and steam bent. Over the centuries, as the wood has dried out, the flyer has opened and is now too wide to clear the mother-of-all when turned. This has been a well made and very heavy wheel.

HEIGHT: 41 in.
DEPTH: 24 in.
LENGTH: 33 in.

WHEEL NO. 30

WHEEL NO. 31

This heavy English or Irish wheel would appear to have been made in the late eighteenth century. The proportions are very reminiscent of the Arkwright wheel pictured in Patricia Baines' book *Spinning Wheels, Spinners and Spinning*. It is solid and heavy with massive turnings.

There is one hole in the table to hold the distaff. The wheel support braces come from the legs. The treadle is attached to the treadle bar by an elaborate wooden moulding.

HEIGHT: 41 in.
DEPTH: 18 in.
LENGTH: 32 in.

WHEEL NO. 31

WHEEL NO. 32

This wheel most likely comes from England. It has been suggested that it was first a hand turned bobbin-flyer wheel and that the treadle was added later. Certainly it has a very pleasant utilitarian handle on the wheel (visible on the left mid-side of the wheel in the photograph.) If this was so, it was probably made in the very early eighteenth century.

It is equipped with a bobbin brake (Scottish tension). The treadle is an unusual shape. The wheel is well made and has an aura of elegance.

HEIGHT: 40 in.
DEPTH: 19 in.
LENGTH: 35 in.

WHEEL NO. 32

WHEEL NO. 33

This wheel comes from Finland and has the characteristic arched double wheel supports. Judging from the size of the orifice it was used for spinning wool as well as flax. There is one place for a distaff. The treadle is gracefully shaped and attached to the treadle bar by wooden pegs. The turnings are simple and the only decoration is the beaded edge on the table.

HEIGHT: 35.5 in.
DEPTH: 22 in.
LENGTH: 38.5

WHEEL NO. 33

WHEEL NO. 34

This early nineteenth century wheel is probably Scandinavian judging by the slope of the table and general proportions.

Carved into the end of the table, each side of the tensioning screw, are the initials "A.C.S.S." In front of the wheel supports on the table is painted a decorative strip, red and green, on which is carved the date 1818 and the initials "B.A.S." It is thought that initials appearing on the end of the spinning wheel tables are those of the maker, while initials placed prominently on the top of the table are those of the owner.

There is one place to carry a distaff. The treadle is nailed to the treadle bar. The end of the table bearing the tensioning screw is beautifully shaped and sculptured.

Much care and pride seems to have been taken in the making of this wheel.

HEIGHT: 34.5 in.
DEPTH: 19 in.
LENGTH: 36 in.

WHEEL NO. 34

WHEEL NO. 35

This is a beautifully built wheel, thought to be European. The turnings and shapes used in the upper longitudinal bars and the mother-of-all are most unusual. It has a metal flyer, the arms of which are notched to carry the thread along the bobbin. There is no place to carry a distaff. The wheel appears to have been much used.

HEIGHT:	30 in.
DEPTH:	13 in.
LENGTH:	33 in.

WHEEL NO. 35

WHEEL NO. 36

This is a strange wheel about which nothing is known. It does not appear to be American. The wheel is turned by hand. There is no tensioning device, but the mother-of-all can be slid along the post to get a satisfactory line up with the wheel. A Scottish tensioner (bobbin drag) is used. The wheel is hand turned by its handle. The orifice is small, suitable for spinning flax.

HEIGHT: 28.5 in.
DEPTH: 19.5 in.
LENGTH: 27.5 in.

WHEEL NO. 36

WHEEL NO. 37

This wheel, probably from the nineteenth century, was made in Turkey. The posts supporting the back wheel have been gnawed by rats trying to get at the grease around the axle. It is a well made, well finished wheel.

The maidens, mother-of-all, tension screw, legs and wheel supports are turned in a very disciplined manner and decorated with rope burn adornment. In addition the maidens and mother-of-all have "captive rings" (free floating rings). These may have been turned from sheer exuberance, an artisans joy and pride in his ability, or they may have been included as an amulet.

There are two places to the left of the mother-of-all for a distaff carrier and a water container. The holes in the table between the flyer and the wheels appear to be purely decorative.

The spinner sat on the ground to spin and turned the wheel by hand.

HEIGHT: 19.5 in.
DEPTH: 19 in.
LENGTH: 36 in.

WHEEL NO. 37

WHEEL NO. 38

This is a table model horizontal bobbin-flyer wheel made in England in the late eighteenth century.

The wooden base has been hollowed out and filled with lead to give it weight. This makes clamping it to a table unnecessary. The wheel is turned by the handle (knob missing) on the axle. The tensioning device is the traditional screw, passing through the end of the table into the mother-of-all block.

The turnings are fine and intricate without being fussy. The wheel rim is lead, half an inch thick and three quarters of an inch wide, which gives it a splendid momentum. The table has a decorative edging of veneer, and a circular inlay of a different wood, which is bordered by two rows of tracery. The distaff carrier has a hole for a water vessel holder about two inches from the distaff.

The distaff appears to be original.

HEIGHT: 10.25 in.
DEPTH: 7 in.
LENGTH: 17 in.

WHEEL NO. 38

European
Vertical
Bobbin-Flyer
Wheels

WHEEL NO. 39

This wheel probably came from north east Europe and was made in the early nineteenth or late eighteenth century.

The outstanding feature of this vertical wheel is its enormous bobbin-flyer and whorl. The rest of the wheel is of quite modest proportions with a T-shaped table and a hexagonal tensioner handle.

The orifice end of the flyer rests in a wood support where is secured by a half-inch wide leather strip. The distaff bar has three positions for the distaff; undoubtedly one held a water container. The treadle is attached to the treadle bar by leather hinges. The treadle is a roughly made obvious replacement.

WHEEL NO. 39

WHEEL NO. 40

This wheel very likely came from the Ukraine and is also a late eighteenth or early nineteenth century product. The distaff may or may not be original, but it is typical of the type of distaff used in Russia with these wheels. The turnings are simple and the wheel is well made. The tensioner is larger and more elaborate than those usually found on this type of wheel. The bobbin-flyer and whorl, like those of other wheels of this style, are large and bulky.

HEIGHT: 39 in.
DEPTH: 16 in.
WIDTH: 21 in.

WHEEL NO. 40

WHEEL NO. 41

Again, this small Ukrainian wheel is probably from the eighteenth or early nineteenth century.

The position of the T shaped table is reversed from its usual direction (compare with wheels 40 and 42) The treadle is fitted into the treadle bar. The tensioner is very nicely shaped. Red and green stripes have been painted on every part of the wheel. Although this paint is probably twentieth century, it does not appear to be very recent. It can be imagined that someone had the urge to give this wheel a "face lift."

HEIGHT: 35 in.
DEPTH: 15 in.
WIDTH: 19 in.

WHEEL NO. 41

WHEEL NO. 42

Slightly smaller than wheel 43 and showing finer craftsmanship than wheel 44, this is another eighteenth or early nineteenth century wheel from northeast Europe.

There are two places for a distaff, the second being in the back of the table. One probably held the water cup for spinning flax. This wheel, after spending many years stored in a New England chicken house was brought to light in 1970. The manure was scraped off it, the tensioning mechanism, which was worn out, was replaced and the wheel was used for spinning once again.

HEIGHT: 38.5 in.
DEPTH: 15.5 in.
WIDTH: 19 in.

WHEEL NO. 42

WHEEL NO. 43

This is another late eighteenth or early nineteenth century wheel from Poland, eastern Germany or Russia. It has a round table, no turnings, and the same massive bobbin-flyer and whorl as wheels 39 and 41. There is no place for a distaff to be carried on the wheel.

HEIGHT: 36 in.
DEPTH: 15 in.
WIDTH: 16 in.

WHEEL NO. 43

WHEEL NO. 44

This type of wheel usually comes from the Ukraine or surrounding areas. This one has an octagonal table. It is solid and well made, built to last. There is at present old yellow paint on it, but where the paint is beginning to wear off a very dark red paint can be seen. There is no place for a distaff carrier.

HEIGHT: 40 in.
DEPTH: 17 in.
WIDTH: 22 in.

WHEEL NO. 44

WHEEL NO. 45

This is another wheel from northeast Europe, most likely built in the mid or early nineteenth century.

Its unusual feature is the metal flyer which instead of being notched has hooks made by bending very heavy wire around the arms of the flyer. It is not quite clear whether the hooks are soldered to the arms, as well as wrapped around them. The distaff carrier is attached to the mother-of-all. there is also a place in the back cross bar of the table to carry the distaff or a water cup.

HEIGHT: 34 in.
DEPTH: 13 in.
WIDTH: 18.5 in.

WHEEL NO. 45

WHEEL NO. 46

This is another Eastern European wheel, resembling wheel no. 42 with it's "T" shaped table and very bulky flyer. However in this case the flyer is supported by horizontal maidens, to the right of the mother-of-all. The tensioning device is a long metal threaded rod with a winged metal nut. There is only one place for a distaff carrier. The wheel is very thick and heavy. It probably dates in the last half of the nineteenth century.

HEIGHT: 37.5 in.
DEPTH: 15 in.
WIDTH: 16 in.

WHEEL NO. 46

WHEEL NO. 47

This upright wheel is probably from Poland or East Germany. Here the maidens are carried horizontally, and the flyer lies to the right of the wheel axle. The flyer is metal and the thread is passed along the bobbin by placing it in the notches on the metal arms. The treadle is a most unusual shape and seems awkward, however, it does work. The wheel is simple and well made.

HEIGHT: 35 in.
DEPTH: 17 in.
WIDTH: 19 in.

WHEEL NO. 47

WHEEL NO. 48

This is a solid chunky "no nonsense" wheel thought to have been built in Switzerland or western Germany in the early nineteenth century.

The table is a sideways "T." The uprights are thick and sturdy, the wheel heavy. The octagonal spokes of the wheel appear to have been hand shaped. A single thick wood screw passes into the mother-of-all for tensioning the single driving band. There is no whorl on the flyer. Instead the left maiden is hinged and fitted with a screw peg. By tightening this screw the flyer can be slowed (Flyer brake). The treadle is on the outside and to the left of the frame. The only decorations are the deep grooves in the tension bar, maidens, mother-of-all and uprights.

HEIGHT:	34 in.
DEPTH:	19 in.
WIDTH:	21 in.

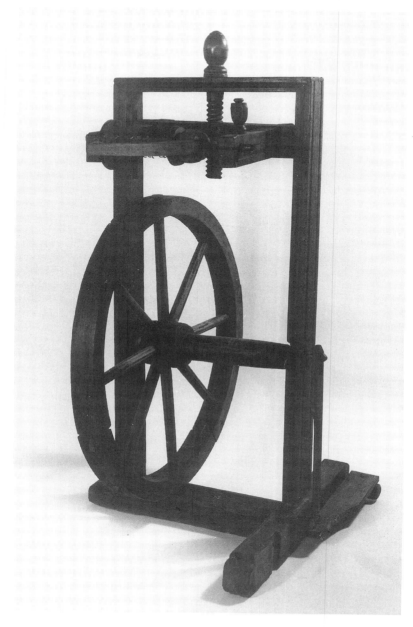

WHEEL NO. 48

EUROPEAN VERTICAL BOBBIN-FLYER WHEELS / III

WHEEL NO. 49

This wheel is thought to be of German origin, probably made in the late eighteenth or early nineteenth century. It is a different type wheel in its overall appearance, having many features in common with wheel no. 53. Again, the solid uprights which support the wheel, the mother-of-all and finally the tensioning mechanism arise from a stable four sided base.

The wheel is small in diameter but thick and heavy, giving it good momentum. The flyer arm (one is broken off) is almost "L" shaped and instead of hooks to carry the thread, has holes along it. A metal eye would have been moved along these holes. There is no whorl. Instead the orifice end of the flyer fits through a leather strip placed between two wooden pieces on the maiden. The upper wooden piece is fitted into a notch in the lower wooden piece and a hinge is formed by a small wooden peg. A large wooden peg passing through these wooden pieces, close to the orifice, can be screwed to loosen or tighten the pressure on the flyer (flyer brake). Two magnificent, large screws pass through the mother-of-all to adjust the tension on the driving band.

The treadle is outside and to the right of the frame.

The only decoration is some sedate grooving on the tensioner bar mother-of-all, maidens and uprights.

HEIGHT: 31.5 in.
DEPTH: 17.5 in.
WIDTH: 19 in.

WHEEL NO. 49

WHEEL NO. 50

This wheel came from a small village in the Black Forest, brought to the U.S.A. by a soldier returning after World War II. Unfortunately the bobbin-flyer assembly was lost during its various travels. The wheel was probably made in the late eighteenth century.

The table is "L" shaped and two inches from the ground. From it arise two long tapering rods. These hold the wheel, and then continue up to carry the mother-of-all, and finally end in the bar that bears the tensioning screw. These rods slope in towards each other as they ascend. The treadle is on the outside, to the left, of the frame. A drag was used on the flyer. The peg to adjust it still remains.

The wheel spokes and the tension screw have a most modest turning. Grooves on the table uprights and maidens are the only other decoration. There is no place for a distaff.

HEIGHT: 36.75 in.
DEPTH: 28 in.
WIDTH: 14 in.

WHEEL NO. 50

WHEEL NO. 51

This is a wheel made with love, probably in Switzerland and comes as a delight after the stolidness of wheels 49 and 50.

Two tapering uprights, with carved "windows" at the bottom, arise from the four sided base. Again, the uprights carry the wheel, the mother-of-all and across the top the bar that holds the tensioning screw. The treadle is on the left and outside of the frame. The flyer has a whorl and does not use the Scottish tensioning system. The flyer is held in place by two attractively carved thin flat pieces of wood, through each of which passes a screw fitted knob. By loosening the knobs the restraining flat pieces may be swung to the side and the bobbin-flyer assembly removed.

The spokes are tapered and have modest turnings. The uprights and mother-of-all have groove decoration. The ends of the mother-of-all and the tension bar have chip carving. The top tension bar has a lovely nail punch decoration of flowers and geometric design; at the left end is a small cross. On the back of the mother-of-all, the date 1851 is nail punched.

HEIGHT: 35 in.
DEPTH: 18 in.
WIDTH: 23 in.

WHEEL NO. 51

WHEEL NO. 52

This wheel, so similar in construction to wheel 51 is reputedly from Switzerland and was probably built in the early nineteenth century.

Again two uprights support the wheel, the mother-of-all and the bar for the tensioning screw. The maidens are horizontal. The flyer has a brake, tightened by a peg in the maiden. The "table" is L shaped and the treadle is outside on the left. There is no place for a distaff.

The turnings on the mother-of-all, the bar supporting the tensioning screw, and the tension screw itself are intricate and beautiful. Its crowning glory is the wooden winged nut on the tensioning screw, carved in the shape of a sheep's heads.

HEIGHT: 39 in.
DEPTH: 27.5 in.
WIDTH: 27 in.

WHEEL NO. 52

WHEEL NO. 53

This is a very unusual wheel thought to be mid nineteenth century, from Germany or England. The arrangement of the bobbin-flyer assembly extending on the spindle in front of the maidens is known as a "Picardy" wheel.

The maidens on this wheel are brass and equipped with small oil holes. The flyer is metal with notches to carry the thread along the bobbin. The wheel edge is leaded to give it extra weight for smooth turning. Over the lead is a fine piece of tin sheet shaped into two grooves for the driving band. The bobbin speed is regulated by a Scottish tensioner (a drag on the bobbin). There is one place in the table to hold a distaff.

The wheel displays sophisticated craftsmanship and beautiful wood.

HEIGHT:	38 in.
DEPTH:	11.5 in.
WIDTH:	18.5 in.

WHEEL NO. 53

WHEEL NO. 54

Like wheel 53, this is a Picardy wheel with the bobbin-flyer assembly extending in front of the maidens instead of between them. A bobbin drag controls its rate of twist.

When purchased this wheel had lost one leg, the treadle, and the bobbin-flyer assembly. However, since Picardy wheels are so rare it seemed worthwhile to replace the missing parts. The original wheel was painted a soft blue with cream trim. The paint appears relatively old — but who knows? There is a screw at the back of the rear wheel post that can be used to align the whorl. There is also a tensioning device at the top of the rear wheel post for adjusting the drive band.

HEIGHT: 38 in.
DEPTH: 11.5 in.
WIDTH: 16 in.

WHEEL NO. 54

WHEEL NO. 55

This wheel is known to have been brought to the United States from Florence, Italy. It was probably made in the late nineteenth century.

The flyer is made of metal with L shaped arms. A rigid ring on a thumbscrew can be slid along the flyer arm to fill the bobbin. There is no whorl; instead a leather strap across the flyer behind the orifice can be loosened or tightened (flyer brake). A metal screw in the right hand maiden allows the tension on the single drive band from the wheel to the bobbin groove to be adjusted. There is no place to carry a distaff.

HEIGHT: 30 in.
DEPTH: 30 in.
WIDTH: 17 in.

WHEEL NO. 55

WHEEL NO. 56

This wheel is usually known as "The Irish Castle Wheel." However, in the Pennsylvania Dutch Country, these wheels are called German wheels or sometimes corner wheels. Also a visitor to the collection said she knew a family in New York who, three generations ago, brought just such a wheel with them when they came from Germany to America. Similar wheels were made in many Irish settlements in America. In Pennsylvania there were several makers; they are also known to have been made in Derry, New Hampshire.

The wheel photographed here is thought to have been brought to this country by immigrants. It is heavier and chunkier than those made in America. Also the ones made in this country usually have a bar joining the two front legs, just below the mother-of-all. In the bar that carries the front wheel support is a hole for the distaff carrier and another hole for the water vessel. This wheel is completely worn out from use.

HEIGHT: 42 in.
DEPTH: 16 in.
WIDTH: 21.5 in.

WHEEL NO. 56

WHEEL NO. 57

This wheel reputedly came from Scandinavia. It is primitively made and it has been suggested that it dates from the time of the First World War.

The lazy Kate at the back of the frame is adjustable and held in place by a peg that fits through the stem and into the upper cross piece of the frame. The flyer is made by a crosspiece into which two straight wood arms are tongue and grooved. The spokes of the wheel are hand whittled. The maidens are mounted on a frame fitted on runners and can be slid back and forth to line up with the wheel. Its position is secured by a large metal thumb screw. On the left hand side of the upper frame a brass bullet shell, 1-and-5/16th-inch diameter, is mounted. It was perhaps used as a water cup when flax was spun.

HEIGHT:	30.5 in.
DEPTH:	16.5 in.
WIDTH:	16.25 in.

WHEEL NO. 57

WHEEL NO. 58

This wheel is thought to have been made in England around the end of the eighteenth century. It has a very unusual mechanism for filling the bobbin without using hooks on the flyer.

There are two horizontal bars above the wheel. The top one carries the maidens which hold the flyer and the bobbin. The bar is hollow and has an open three and a half inch slot. A small block of wood bearing a tongue that reaches up into the lower side of the bobbin whorl is inserted into this slot. (Also from this block is a bobbin drag, the tension of which in controlled by the peg inserted in the block side.) Through the bar and the block a wooden screw passes, ending in a handle just below the orifice. When this handle is turned, the block moves along the wooden screw and, because of the tongue in the bobbin whorl, the bobbin is pulled along the bobbin-flyer axle. The flyer, which is fixed at the front end of the axle, carries the thread from the orifice, through a ring at the front of the arm, then through a notch at the end of the arm. As the spinner spins she turns the screw handle at intervals and the bobbin is pushed along the axle into the flyer receiving the thread from the flyer arm as it passes. This mechanism makes it possible for the spinner to spin continuously without stopping to change the position of the thread. One might say this is the fore runner of the modern "woolie winder." The wheel is probably from the same era as the Doughty Wheel. (*The Encyclopedia of Hand Spinning* by Mabel Ross).

The whole machine is beautifully made. The wheel rim is filled with lead to give it momentum. The turnings are restrained and elegant. The lower horizontal bar is fitted with a vertical wooden screw which levels the upper bar. The drive band tension is adjusted by a screw in the back wheel support. A little ivory finial decorates this screw and the lower horizontal bar.

HEIGHT:	35 in.
DEPTH:	17 in.
WIDTH:	17 in.

WHEEL NO. 58

American Wheels

WHEEL NO. 59

This wheel, made in the late eighteenth or early nineteenth century is a typical New Hampshire wheel of that time. The wide rim, the wheel posts protruding well below the table, the well spread legs and the overall dimensions are similar to the Shaker wheels of this period. There are simple turnings on the maidens and legs. This wheel is signed "Ramsey."

HEIGHT: 34 in.
DEPTH: 22 in.
LENGTH: 35 in.

WHEEL NO. 59

WHEEL NO. 60

This Shaker wheel is signed "T.C.," thought to be Thomas Cushman, the deacon of the Shaker community at Alfred, Maine. Initials on Shaker wheels are often the stamp of approval of the community, not the initials of the particular man who made it. The most distinguishing features of Shaker wheels are the overall dimensions, the simplicity of the finials and the lack of turnings, the width of the wheel rim, and the wide spread, elegantly shaped legs.

HEIGHT: 34.25 in.
DEPTH: 24.5 in.
LENGTH: 35 in.

WHEEL NO. 60

WHEEL NO. 61

This is another Shaker wheel bearing all the characteristics mentioned in wheel no. 60. This one bears the initials "F.W." for Francis Winkley, deacon at the Canterbury, New Hampshire, Shaker community in the very early nineteenth century. It is interesting to note how far below the table the wheel posts protrude; also, that the posts have no braces from the table or the legs. However these wheels are usually as strong and stable, with no warping of the wheel, as they were when made, nearly two hundred years ago.

HEIGHT: 34 in.
DEPTH: 23 in.
LENGTH: 34 in.

WHEEL NO. 61

WHEEL NO. 62

This wheel, with simple turnings, would appear to be, in every respect, a typical New England wheel of the late eighteenth or early nineteenth century, except for its enormous bobbin-flyer assembly. It is thought that the fourteen inch mother-of-all and the thirteen inch flyer were put on the wheel at a later date. Evidently some lady in the past objected to interrupting her spinning to change the bobbin as frequently as required with a standard sized bobbin. The lack of a place for a distaff carrier, together with the large orifice, suggests that the wheel was used primarily for spinning wool.

HEIGHT: 35 in.
DEPTH: 19 in.
LENGTH: 31.5 in.

WHEEL NO. 62

WHEEL NO. 63

This wheel is signed "L. Brown" on the edge and on the end of the table. L. Brown was a wheel maker in upper state New York (Taylor and Pennington, verbal communication).

The design, like wheel no. 67, shows a German influence. The mother-of-all is supported on two posts attached to the front table sides by wooden screws. Tension on the drive band is controlled by the threaded rod which passes through the mother-of-all into the front wheel post. There is no place for a distaff carrier. This wheel was probably made in the early nineteenth century.

HEIGHT: 35 in.
DEPTH: 12.5 in.
LENGTH: 24 in.

WHEEL NO. 63

WHEEL NO. 64

This wheel is thought to have been made in the United States during the nineteenth century, but its design has a strong German influence.

The small upper table, on two posts, supports the mother-of-all, the position of which can be adjusted by the traditional tensioning screw passing through the end of the table into the mother-of-all block. Two threaded stretchers pass from the other end of the table into the wheel supports. These stabilize the posts and allow adjustment in lining up the wheel.

On the primary table are two posts, three inches tall, each equipped with a small hole two inches above the table. The two posts supporting the small table also have a small hole in them, six inches above their base. There have been two suggestions as to their original use: perhaps a bar, inserted between the posts, held extra bobbins, or inserted bars may have formed a crib to hold rolags.

There is one place for a distaff carrier.

HEIGHT: 33.75 in.
DEPTH: 14 in.
LENGTH: 36 in.

No. 65 has been withdrawn.

WHEEL NO. 64

WHEEL NO. 66

The lines and dimensions of this wheel are the same as those of the Shaker wheels and the common New Hampshire wheel. The shaping of the wheel posts and legs and the beading around the table edge however make it unlikely to be a Shaker wheel.

Its interesting feature is the maidens which end in little onion domes. The double flyer wheel, no. 106, was obviously made by the same hand. Although several double flyer wheels of this design have been seen, this is the only single flyer wheel found so far.

HEIGHT: 33.5 in.
DEPTH: 23.5 in.
LENGTH: 33.5 in.

WHEEL NO. 66

WHEEL NO. 67

This wheel may be American, Scottish, or Canadian. The dimensions are larger than most Scottish wheels; unlike most Canadian wheels it has a place for a distaff carrier; American wheels do not as a rule use a Scottish tensioner. (bobbin brake).

The wheel support posts, the mother-of-all and the legs are chunky. The spokes are fixed to the wheel rim with wooden pegs. Wheel turnings are simple. There is one wheel support brace which goes from the table to the wheel post bearing the jackman. The treadle back board is harp shaped. In addition to the Scottish tension there is the traditional screw tension through the table end. There is one place for a distaff carrier.

HEIGHT: 41.5 in.
DEPTH: 19 in.
LENGTH: 40 in.

WHEEL NO. 67

WHEEL NO. 68

The proportions and the very sloped table of this wheel are similar to those of wheels frequently found in Scandinavia. When the wheel was purchased it was said to have been made by a Scandinavian man, living in Wisconsin, about the middle of the nineteenth century.

The wheel support posts are deeply inserted through the table, and are further stabilized by the braces which arise from the legs. The legs penetrate deeply into the end of the table. The turnings are minimal. The treadle is a graceful shape. The wheel has been painted with what appears to be very old red paint.

HEIGHT: 29.25 in.
DEPTH: 17 in.
LENGTH: 39 in.

WHEEL NO. 68

WHEEL NO. 69

This wheel came from a farm house in central New Hampshire. It resembles the common New Hampshire wheel (see wheel no. 63, 64, 68) of the early nineteenth and late eighteenth centuries. However, it is slightly smaller in every dimension which gives it a very refined appearance.

The wheel posts, maidens and distaff holder are turned with restraint. The table has well executed beading and chip carving. The legs are widely spread and contoured like those found on Shaker wheels, until they shape out for the foot. It is an unusually carefully made wheel and bears the signature "Hatch."

HEIGHT: 32 in.
DEPTH: 24 in.
LENGTH: 32 in.

WHEEL NO. 69

WHEEL NO. 70

This wheel came from the mid-western United States and was purchased in Massachusetts.

The wheel, legs and treadle bar, all of which have good turnings, are out of keeping with the primitive construction of the frame. They probably were from another wheel originally. Four knobs at the top of the frame unscrew, allowing removal of the transverse bars and hence the wheel. These transverse bars, one and a half inches wide where the screw knobs go, are cut away to half an inch wide. Evidently the wheel was a little too large for the frame as first measured. The tensioning mechanism is the same as commonly found on northeastern European wheels. (See wheels no. 44, 45, & 46.)

HEIGHT: 37.25 in.
DEPTH: 13 in.
WIDTH: 23.5 in.

WHEEL NO. 70

WHEEL NO. 71

These wheels, known as "Connecticut Chair Wheels" are an American invention of the early nineteenth century supposedly first made in Connecticut by a chair maker. The double treadle and the action of the accelerating wheel allow a slow easy treadling rhythm while spinning.

At the axle a small solid wooden wheel is attached to the upper wheel. A drive band passing around the rim of the lower wheel and the rim of the small solid wheel, transfers the action of the treadle to the large upper wheel. A double drive band passes from the rim of the upper wheel around the bobbin and flyer whorls in the customary manner. The mother-of-all, threaded at each end, passes through the front left hand post where it is secured by a threaded handle. This allows the tension on the double drive band to be easily adjusted. This seems to be the earliest use of a rocker tensioner. There is one place for a distaff carrier placed in the top horizontal bar behind the wheels. This wheel has been ebonized.

HEIGHT: 29 in.
DEPTH: 19 in.
WIDTH: 17.5 in.

WHEEL NO. 71

WHEEL NO. 72

This wheel probably came from Connecticut in the early nineteenth century.

Basically the same as wheel no. 71, this one has a screw adjustment for aligning the upper wheel on the right hand side of the lower and middle horizontal bars. The mother-of-all has its own threaded screw and the tension on the double drive band is adjusted by the rocker method. Since the edge of the lower wheel is smooth, a driving belt instead of the customary cord is used to turn the hub of the upper wheel. The distaff is placed in the middle front, and on the right arm is a hole which undoubtedly supported a water container.

HEIGHT: 32 in.
DEPTH: 18 in.
WIDTH: 19 in.

WHEEL NO. 72

WHEEL NO. 73

This American wheel is similar to the chair wheels but without the frame surrounding it.

Two horizontal bars connected by round posts serve as the table. The left hand post is extended to bear the support for the mother-of-all. The two wheels are carried between the horizontal bars, the lower one being half below and half above and the upper one, (supported by wheel posts arising from the bars) entirely above. Like wheel no. 71, the driving belt passes from the rim of the lower wheel to the hub of the upper wheel. A second double drive band from the outer rim of the upper wheel turns the bobbin and flyer. The mother-of-all ends at the back in a threaded handle. This adjusts the tension on the double driving band. Behind the back horizontal bar is a wooden screw to adjust the tension on the lower driving belt. There is one place for a distaff carrier.

The left front post is signed "B.B."

HEIGHT:	32.25 in.
DEPTH:	19 in.
WIDTH:	20.5 in.

WHEEL NO. 73

WHEEL NO. 74

This basic, primitive wheel was used for spinning hemp for rope making.

The bar of the flyer passes through the solid wheel and is attached to the jackman. There are no whorls, neither on the bobbin or the flyer. Instead a flyer brake is used to create a differential between the turning rate of the bobbin and the flyer.

HEIGHT:	35 in.
DEPTH:	16 in.
WIDTH:	24 in.

WHEEL NO. 74

WHEEL NO. 75

This unusual wheel was probably made in the second half of the nine-teenth century, the era of the patent wheels and American exuberant inventiveness.

The treadles operate with the same motion as the pedals on a paddle boat. The strings pass from the treadle feet to bars above and then over two small pulleys at the front of the cupboard. As the pulleys move they turn the axle of the big solid wheel at the back of the cabinet. A single drive band passes from the outer rim of this big solid wheel are encased in the upper cabinet. Another double drive band passes from the rim of the exposed upper wheel to the bobbin flyer assembly in the usual way. The tension on the driving band connecting the lower and upper wheels is adjusted by the screw in the front wheel support on the table. The tension on the bobbin-flyer band is adjusted by rocker motion of the bobbin-flyer and the desired position stabilized by a wooden screw on the mother-of-all.

The broken distaff may or may not (most probably not) be original but a very similar one would have been used.

HEIGHT: 41 in.
DEPTH: 15 in.
WIDTH: 19 in.

WHEEL NO. 75

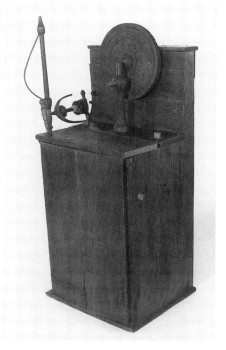

WHEEL NO. 75 CLOSED

WHEEL NO. 76

This American wheel was also built in the last half of the nineteenth century when American inventiveness was rampant.

It is a very plain well built wheel using the accelerating wheel principle and two treadles. The tensioner is the large wood screw which passes through the mother-of-all and a bar connecting the two wheel support posts. The method of transfering the action of the second treadle to the footman is unique and ingenious. Several wheels of this design are known to be still in existence.

HEIGHT   35 in.
DEPTH: 13 in.
WIDTH: 14.75 in.

WHEEL NO. 76

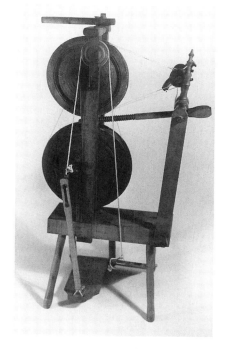

WHEEL NO. 76, BACK

WHEEL NO. 77

This wheel, known as the Webster Yarn Maker, was patented in 1934. It was made to be screwed onto a table.

The mechanism is ingenious. When the handle is pushed in and turned the bobbin alone turns, and twist is put into the drawn out fibres. When the draw and twist are completed, the handle is pulled out and turned in the same direction. This engages a gear which turns the frame holding the bobbin and the thread is drawn on.

HEIGHT: 6 in.
DEPTH: 4 in.
LENGTH: 6.75 in.

WHEEL NO. 77

Canadian Wheels

WHEEL NO. 78

This is a very old Canadian hand turned wheel from the early eighteenth century. Since it is equipped with a bar for a bobbin brake, it is assumed that it was a bobbin-flyer wheel. Although primitive in some respects, the turnings show the work of a good craftsman.

HEIGHT: 43 in.
DEPTH: 15 in.
LENGTH: 43 in.

WHEEL NO. 78

WHEEL NO. 79

This eighteenth century Canadian wheel was a common design in its time. Today most of them are found converted to quillers.

The wheel has an ungrooved wide band similar to that found on a spindle wheel. The maidens and the wheel posts penetrate the table by four or five inches. There is no mother-of-all, nor any tensioning mechanism. The turnings and flyer are massive yet elegant. This particular wheel lacks its whorl and footman.

HEIGHT: 44.5 in.
DEPTH: 20.25 in.
LENGTH: 44.5 in.

WHEEL NO. 79

WHEEL NO. 80

This Canadian wheel was probably made in the early part of the eighteenth century.

All the turnings are nicely executed and pleasantly simple. The spokes are secured into the wheel rim by wooden pegs. The nails used on the frame appear to be hand made. The mounting of the mother-of-all is most unusual. It is held on two posts which originate where the wheel posts enter the table. Braces pass from these posts into the wheel support posts. The bar between the top of the maidens has two holes for pegs. These are aligned with the large, (2.5 in. diameter) metal whorl so that a band from them served as a brake to the spindle. This is the only tensioning device.

Holes in the legs show that at sometime there was a treadle. This could have been a later addition.

HEIGHT:	39 in.
DEPTH:	19 in.
LENGTH:	33.75 in.

WHEEL NO. 80

WHEEL NO. 81

This Canadian wheel was probably made in the eighteenth or very early nineteenth century.

The wheel has a broad ungrooved band similar to those on spindle wheels. All the turnings are simple; the lower legs are chamfered. The braces of the wheel supports are in front and fastened into the table. The more usual position of the braces is behind the posts and fastened into the end of the table. The table has three holes, perhaps one for a distaff (although this is rare on Canadian wheels), one for a water container, and one for the tensioning mechanism.

The tensioning mechanism is of the rocker type. A large wooden handle penetrates the mother-of-all and fits through an opening in the table. At the bottom of the handle is a hole with the remains of a piece of cord. It is thought that this cord passed from the handle through one of the holes in the table where it was secured by a wooden peg.

The flyer of this wheel is missing.

HEIGHT: 42.5 in.
DEPTH: 16 in.
LENGTH: 46.5 in.

WHEEL NO. 81

WHEEL NO. 82

This is a Quebec wheel, older than wheels nos. 92, 93, and 94, probably made in the first half of the eighteenth century.

The tensioning mechanism is the traditional wooden screw, passing through the end of the table into the block which carries the mother-of-all. There is only one wheel support brace which goes from the table to the back support brace. Like most Canadian wheels it has no place for a distaff carrier.

HEIGHT: 41.5 in.
DEPTH: 19 in.
LENGTH: 42 in.

WHEEL NO. 82

WHEEL NO. 83

This old Quebec wheel, probably from the late eighteenth or early nineteenth century, was very well made.

The turnings on the spokes, supports, legs, and mother-of-all and maidens are simple and pleasing. Both wheel supports are braced from the table. The flyer is an unusual shape, flattened and cut from one piece of wood. The treadle is gracefully shaped. There is no place for a distaff carrier.

HEIGHT: 37 in.
DEPTH: 18.5 in.
LENGTH: 40 in.

WHEEL NO. 83

WHEEL NO. 84

This small wheel, purchased in Vermont, is thought to have come from Canada. It is probably from the late eighteenth or early nineteenth century. It has a coat of very deep red paint that gives it a cheerful air.

There are no post braces. The usual traditional screw tensioner is used. The attachment of the footman to the treadle is unusual. A large peg is inserted into the treadle and through this peg a small peg passes into the footman. There is no place for a distaff carrier.

HEIGHT: 35.5 in.
DEPTH: 23 in.
LENGTH: 33 in.

WHEEL NO. 84

WHEEL NO. 85

Wheels of these dimensions are commonly found in Nova Scotia, and in Scotland, and several have been seen in the Boston area, thought to have been brought there by immigrants from Nova Scotia.

It is a compact, well made wheel with simple turnings. The wheel post grooves are lined with copper. The wheel is signed "J.M.Q."

This wheel started the Cummer collection. A New York interior decorator was overheard bargaining with a New Hampshire antique dealer. During their discussion, the decorator remarked, "It won't take a very big pot." It was then realized this lovely little wheel was destined to become a planter in a New York apartment. Obviously, no spinner could tolerate this idea, and so the collection began.

HEIGHT: 36 in.
DEPTH: 23 in.
LENGTH: 33 in.

WHEEL NO. 85

WHEEL NO. 86

This ebonized Canadian wheel of compact proportions has a rare bracing of the legs. A metal rod joining the two back legs passes through a
wooden spill which enters the front leg. A similar bracing is seen on
wheel no. 126. There are no braces to the wheel supports. All the turnings are simple and well executed. The wheel was probably made in the
early or mid-nineteenth century.

HEIGHT:	30.5 in.
DEPTH:	18 in.
LENGTH:	36 in.

WHEEL NO. 86

WHEEL NO. 87

This wheel from the Province of Quebec was purchased in Antrim, New Hampshire, from an antique dealer.

The wheel although large is slightly smaller than the usual "Great Canadian" wheels. However, the turnings and the treadle are the same. The wheel supports are not braced as are those of the Great Canadian wheels.

The tensioning mechanism is unique. A metal plate, edged with runners each side, is bolted to the table. Fastened to the mother-of-all is a matching metal plate which fits into the runners. This plate has a large thumb screw at the end. By sliding the mother-of-all plate along the table plate, and securing it in position by the thumb screw, the tension on the single double driving band is easily adjusted.

HEIGHT: 40 in.
DEPTH: 21 in.
LENGTH: 42 in.

WHEEL NO. 87

WHEEL NO. 87, DETAIL

WHEEL NO. 88

These large wheels come from Ste. Hyacinthe, Quebec, where they were made from the last half of the nineteenth century well into the twentieth century. Originally known as "Rouets" wheels, they are commonly referred to as "the Great Canadian Wheel," or recently, in New England, they have been dubbed "Canadian Production Wheels" because of their speed. They usually have approximately a 1:21 ratio between wheel turn and flyer turns.

They are characterized by the large wheel with attractive spoke turnings; a metal clamp rocker tensioner which is easily adjusted by a metal thumb screw; a metal treadle of distinctive design and a metal rod footman. The handle at the table end is not part of the tensioning device. The wheel supports are braced from the table. The table is usually tapered as this one is. These wheels are commonly found to have weathered the years without warp or damage and are in high demand amongst experienced spinners.

HEIGHT: 44 in.
DEPTH: 22 in.
LENGTH: 48 in.

WHEEL NO. 88

WHEEL NO. 89

This wheel is similar to wheel no. 92 in every respect except it has two treadles and its table, of better quality, is finished with decorative beading along the longitudinal edges. The maidens, the wheel supports, and the support braces are more elaborately turned. There are two metal rod footmen.

HEIGHT: 45.5 in.
DEPTH: 22.5 in.
LENGTH: 47 in.

WHEEL NO. 89

WHEEL NO. 90

This Canadian wheel is similar to the "Great Canadian Wheel" (no. 92) in its size, turnings, metal rocker tensioner and metal treadle. However, the table is unusual for these wheels. It is rectangular, with rounded corners at the front and softened corners at the back. Both sides and the front end are beautifully tooled. The overall impression is one of elegance not found in most wheels of this type.

HEIGHT: 45.5 in.
DEPTH: 24 in.
LENGTH: 46.5 in

WHEEL NO. 90

WHEEL NO. 91

This Canadian wheel is signed "Paradis." Judging from the frequency with which they turn up in New England, they must have been a popular wheel. They are always painted a deep butter yellow.

The rocker tensioner is used. The mother-of-all has a wood extension under it which fits into a slot in the table end. A U bolt passes over the mother-of-all into the wood extension on one side, and into the end of the table on the other. The angle of the mother-of-all can be changed by moving the handle that protrudes from it. The position can be secured by a screw nut facing the spinner.

There is no wheel support brace. There is no place for a distaff carrier. The wheel support slots are reinforced with bone.

HEIGHT: 42 in.
DEPTH: 28 in.
LENGTH: 22.5 in.

WHEEL NO. 91

WHEEL NO. 92

This wheel, purchased from a New Hampshire family, was made in Quebec Province. It is very similar to wheel no. 95, but cheaper construction.

There are no finials to the maidens. The turnings are pleasant, but plain. A u-bolt passes over the mother-of-all into a block inserted into an opening in the table. A large bolt passes through the table edges and the block, serving as a pivot for the mother-of-all. By means of the handle attached to it, the position of the mother-of-all can be adjusted. However, there is no means of securing it in position. Nonetheless, when used, there was no slippage and the wheel worked. The jackman has no knob to hold the footman in place. Several of these wheels have been seen and all lacked the knob, which suggests either it was poorly secured, or never existed. A piece of fleece wrapped around the jackman works perfectly well.

The wheel is painted with a mustard paint which appears to be original.

HEIGHT: 40.5 in.
DEPTH: 26 in.
LENGTH: 39.5 in.

WHEEL NO. 92

WHEEL NO. 93

This is the smallest Canadian wheel in the collection.

The wheel itself is one and a half inches thick, which gives it weight and a good momentum. The mother-of-all lies in a wood cradle which is attached to the table. The tensioning system is the rocker type found on wheels from Quebec. A large U bolt extends over the mother-of-all and through the table. Like wheel no. 96 there is no screw or tightening mechanism for the U bolt; however, the mother-of-all stays where placed. In front of the table is a handle, but it has no connection with the rocker tensioner. It is a charming little wheel.

HEIGHT: 31 in.
DEPTH: 23.5 in.
LENGTH: 31 in.

WHEEL NO. 93

WHEEL NO. 94

The overall impression of this wheel is very different from the French Canadian wheels from Quebec, although that is where it came from. It has been suggested that it was made in the more English district known as the Eastern Townships. It is the largest treadle wheel yet found.

The turnings on the spokes, wheel supports, maidens, and legs are elaborate. The mother-of-all is heavy, with deep decorative grooves. Large pegs through the wheel supports steady the wheel axle. Two spokes on the wheel are made from a different wood than the others. It is suggested that the different wood makes these spokes a different weight and this so balances the wheel that, when it stops spinning, it comes to rest with the jackman in position to start turning the wheel when treadled. The table is thick and the longitudinal edges are gracefully contoured. Deep close chip carving completely borders both ends of the table. Also five vertical rows of deep double chip carving decorate the long contoured table edges. The legs are strong, well turned, and shorter than the legs on most Canadian wheels. There is a place for a distaff carrier.

HEIGHT: 52 in.
DEPTH: 21 in.
LENGTH: 54 in.

WHEEL NO. 94

WHEEL NO. 95

This wheel, also from the Province of Quebec, is obviously made by the same man who made wheel no. 98. In every dimension it is a little smaller than wheel no. 34, but still larger than the "Great Canadian" wheels.

The spoke turnings, wheel supports, and braces to the wheel supports are the same as no. 98. The maidens, mother-of-all, and legs are the same turnings but not quite as heavy. The contour of the table is the same. In addition to the same chip carving, this table has trefoil carvings on the edge facing away from the spinner, also a spray of berries. This wheel is not balanced to come to rest in position as does wheel no. 95. The flyer and orifice show wear marks.

HEIGHT: 47 in.
DEPTH: 21 in.
LENGTH: 48 in.

WHEEL NO. 95

WHEEL NO. 96

This Canadian wheel was probably built during the mid to upper nineteenth century when accelerating wheels were in vogue.

The center table is cut away so that the primary driving wheel is equally below and above the table, its axle resting on metal holders attached to the table. The jackman has two bends to accept the two footmen from the two treadles. The upper wheel has a small solid wheel (or perhaps a greatly enlarged hub) attached to the back axle. A single driving belt goes around this upper solid wheel and down around the rim of the lower wheel. A separate double driving band goes from the rim of the full sized upper wheel to the bobbin flyer assembly. All this is very comparable to the Connecticut chair wheels (no. 71 and 72).

The bobbin-flyer assembly is unusual in that the grooves of the whorl are smaller than the groove of the bobbin. The mother-of-all is cradled on the table and secured by a large U bolt which passes over it and through the table. This gives a rocker tensioning mechanism. A handle at the end of the table has broken off. The turnings are simple and pleasing. It is a well made wheel.

HEIGHT: 35 in.
DEPTH: 18.5 in.
LENGTH: 25 in.

WHEEL NO. 96

WHEEL NO. 97

This horizontal wheel was made in Canada in the second half of the nineteenth century.

The two treadles connect to the S shaped axle of the lower wheel. By using a single belt the drive from this wheel passes to the hub of the upper wheel. A single double drive band from the outer rim of the upper wheel drives the bobbin and the flyer. Tensioning is accomplished by the traditional screw through the table end. Like the chair wheels, this wheel allows the spinner to achieve good turning speed with relaxed treadling.

HEIGHT: 37.5 in.
DEPTH: 18 in.
LENGTH: 36 in.

WHEEL NO. 97

WHEEL NO. 98

This metal Canadian wheel, found in Newfoundland, appears to have been built to the patent of Vigeant and Desmarets issued in Canada in 1880. (*Selected Canadian Spinning Wheels in Perspective* by Judith Buxton-Keenlyside.)

The whole wheel is metal except for the bobbin and the treadle, which appear to be original. At some point the actual wheel has fractured, and been welded carefully. Fragility undoubtedly was a problem for these cast wheels.

A spring loaded screw holds the bobbin in place, and tension is adjusted by a screw below the mother-of-all. The outer edge of the wheel has a tin capping with two grooves, one slightly deeper than the other. The hooks on the flyer have disintegrated on this wheel, but appear to have been made from wound wire judging from what remains of them. The overall appearance of the wheel has a grace to it that makes it quite attractive.

HEIGHT: 38.5 in.
DEPTH: 19.5 in.
LENGTH: 33.5 in.

WHEEL NO. 98

WHEEL NO. 99

This wheel, while not antique, is of historical interest.

It consists of a very large flyer, 17 inches long with an orifice of 0.75 inches in diameter. The maidens are mounted on a board long enough to bridge the old working area of the Singer sewing treadle machine. At the base of the front maiden is a small block of wood with a peg. This allows the use of a flyer brake. The head is lined up and driven by the treadle powered wheel of the sewing machine.

These wheels were popular with the Salish Indians at Cowichan Bay on Vancouver Island during the nineteen-fifties and sixties. By the nineteen seventies, electric sewing machines were adapted to drive the bobbin. The wheel is especially suited for spinning the bulky yarn used in Cowichan sweaters. However, since heads made in Australia were purchasable in Victoria, B.C., it has been suggested that the adaptation of the sewing machines may have originated in that country.

HEIGHT: 38.5 in.
DEPTH: 17.25 in.
LENGTH: 36 in

WHEEL NO. 99

WHEEL NO. 100

This wheel is thought to have been made by the Spin-Well Co., in Sifton, Manitoba. During the Great Depression of the 1930s these wheels were very popular in the western provinces of Canada.

The wheel is solid metal (some sort of lead amalgam from the appearance), with a metal axle. The flyer is also made from the same metal. A block of wood with a screw ending in a winged nut fits into a slot in the back vertical wheel support. Moving this block adjusts the tension on the drive board.

The treadle is a straight board, seven inches wide, pivoted into the front legs. On the right hand side of the frame is a lazy Kate held in place by a firmly attached metal clamp. A small hook on the side of the right front wheel support undoubtedly held a threading hook. The wheel is simply but nicely made.

HEIGHT: 21.25 in.
DEPTH: 16 in.
LENGTH: 19.25 in.

WHEEL NO. 100

Double Flyer Wheels

WHEEL NO. IOI

This American double flyer wheel is a design made in the early to mid-nineteenth century by several makers in Connecticut and Pennsylvania. This one is signed "S. Barnum."

Both flyers are the same height and distance from the wheel, and each has its own tensioner. Engineers claim it must have used two double drive bands. Why else would the maker go to the trouble of making two tensioners? Most spinners feel that a single double drive band was used, turning both flyers at the same speed. for this the second tensioner is unnecessary.

This wheel has a nail crossing the bottom of the wheel support groove to prevent wear on the post. It is sturdy and well-made.

HEIGHT: 30.5 in.
DEPTH: 17 in.
WIDTH: 17 in.

WHEEL NO. 101

DOUBLE FLYER WHEELS / 221

WHEEL NO. 102

This double flyer wheel was probably made in New England in the early nineteenth century.

Its unique feature is the positioning of the two tensioning screws, one at each end of the table, in the traditional manner used in single bobbin-flyer wheels. Again the question arises: Were one or two double driving bands used? There are two broad grooves in the wheel. Both flyers are in identical positions in relation to the wheel.

The turnings on the legs and maidens are very simple. The only decoration on the table is a double beading along the front and back edges. The wheel support grooves are lined with copper to prevent wear on the posts. The treadle is fitted into and nailed to the treadle board.

HEIGHT: 47 in.
DEPTH: 17 in.
WIDTH: 27 in.

WHEEL NO. 102

WHEEL NO. 103

This is a double flyer wheel with a single tensioner, thought to have been made in Connecticut or upper New York State during the first half of the nineteenth century.

The tensioning rod passes from the table to the bar which carries the short wheel supports. It is threaded for about eight inches when it passes through the bar carrying both mother-of-alls. At present the tensioning rod has seized up at both ends and cannot be turned, but even when it was free it seems like an awkward arrangement. Since several wheels like this have been seen, it is thought to have been a relatively common wheel.

The onion-shaped finials are distinctive and attractive.

HEIGHT: 43 in.
DEPTH: 17 in.
WIDTH: 17 in.

WHEEL NO. 103

WHEEL NO. 104

This American double flyer wheel is signed "A. Beers." When it was bought at auction it was said to have been made in Natick, Massachusetts, which may or may not be reliable information.

There is a tensioner for each flyer. The back wheel bushing, but not the front one, is lined with metal. The bottom table has chip carving and decorative grooves along the long edges. The turnings on the spokes, legs, and distaff are extremely simple. It is a very nicely made, nicely finished wheel.

HEIGHT: 44.75 in.
DEPTH: 18.75 in.
WIDTH: 22 in.

WHEEL NO. 104

WHEEL NO. 105

This early nineteenth century American wheel has only one tensioner as wheel 103 has. However on wheel 103 the tension was adjusted by raising or lowering the bobbin-flyer assemblies, but on this one it is accomplished by raising or lowering the actual wheel. The tensioner is the threaded bar which arises from the table and ends in the bar which carries the distaff and the wheel supports. By turning the threaded bar the tension on the single double driving band can be adjusted. Both flyers are equidistant from the wheel axle. The wheel bushings are lined with metal to prevent wear.

HEIGHT: 48 in.
DEPTH: 16 in.
WIDTH: 18 in.

WHEEL NO. 105

WHEEL NO. 106

This horizontal double flyer wheel is probably of Scottish origin.

The wheel itself is a wheel within a wheel, the inner one having twelve spokes and the outer one having twenty-four. The result is a heavy wheel with tremendous momentum. There once were braces from the table to the wheel supports. The maidens are horizontal and parallel. In addition to the standard tensioning mechanism going through the end of the table into the block of the mother-of-all, there is an independent tensioning mechanism on the left end of the back horizontal maiden that changes the left bobbin-flyer assembly. The whorl and one arm of the right flyer is missing. The distaff carrier is on the left back end of the table.

The decoration consists of rope burn lines on the tension handle, maidens, flyers, distaff carrier, and legs; chip carving along both ends of the table, and beading along the table edges. The treadle is fitted into the treadle board and nailed. The whole wheel is massive with simple turnings and beautifully made.

HEIGHT: 36 in.
DEPTH: 25.5 in.
LENGTH: 30 in.

WHEEL NO. 106

WHEEL NO. 107

This small European double flyer wheel was probably made in Switzerland in the mid-nineteenth century. Without elaborate turnings, it is simply but finely constructed. The wheel has two broad grooves and is centered over the table.

At each side of the table there are posts which carry the mother-of-alls and end in a tensioning screw. The left flyer is set higher and further forward than the right flyer (See table of measurements for details.) This accommodates two double driving bands, one for each flyer, which are tensioned separately. The treadle is attached to the treadle board by leather hinge strips.

HEIGHT: 27.5 in.
DEPTH: 14 in.
WIDTH: 19.5 in.

WHEEL NO. 107

DOUBLE FLYER WHEELS / 233

WHEEL NO. 108

This double flyer wheel is also thought to have originated in Switzerland in the early or mid-nineteenth century.

The wheel is off-centre, being placed at the right side of the table and directly over the treadle. The left bobbin-flyer assembly is placed to the left of the wheel axle, whereas the right one is placed directly over the axle. Furthermore the left flyer is slightly more forward and about two inches lower than the right one. (For details, see table of measurements,) Each mother-of-all has its own tensioning device, and the wheel has two broad grooves. Definitely this wheel was made to use two double driving bands.

The turnings are very simple and the wheel is carefully made. The treadle has a small heart carved in it, suggesting that perhaps it was a trousseau wheel. The treadle is attached to the treadle bar by leather hinges.

HEIGHT: 30 in.
DEPTH: 15 in.
WIDTH: 19 in.

WHEEL NO. 108

WHEEL NO. 109

This double-flyer chair wheel is thought to have been made in Connecticut in the early nineteenth century. The overall dimensions are slightly less than those of wheel no. 72.

Both wheels are solid. A flat driving belt passes from the outer rim of the lower wheel over the hub of the upper wheel. The upper wheel has two well-separated grooves suggesting that two double driving bands (one for each flyer) were used.

The whole frame is joined by wooden pegs. Two hand-forged metal thumb screws at the top of the back posts adjust the tension on the drive belt. Tension on the flyer bands is adjusted by rocking the appropriate mother-of-all. Unfortunately, both the original bobbin-flyer assemblies have been lost. The only nails used are square hand-made nails attaching the treadle to the treadle rod.

The turnings on the frame pieces, wheel supports, and maidens are very restrained.

HEIGHT: 27 in.
DEPTH: 20 in.
LENGTH: 21 in.

WHEEL NO. 109

.

Parlor Wheels

WHEEL NO. 110

This is a charming wheel, made probably in the mid-nineteenth century, with wonderful elaborate turnings and finials.

Pewter bands decorate the distaff carrier, and a carved pewter crown is on the back wheel support just before it accepts the tensioning device. The flyer, including the bobbin spindle, is made entirely of wood. Instead of hooks, the flyer arms have holes and a round eye is moved from hole to hole to carry the thread as the bobbin fills. The table is round with a slice cut off to accommodate the spinner's foot. The distaff arises from the table and is joined to the mother-of-all by a turned rod, one and a half inches long, to stabilize it.

HEIGHT: 30 in.
DEPTH: 16.5 in.
WIDTH: 16.5 in.

WHEEL NO. 110

WHEEL NO. III

This small European wheel probably comes from the mid or later nineteenth century.

There are ivory finials at the end of the tensioning screw, the distaff carrier, and the mother-of-all. The tensioning screw and the distaff support have ivory collars. The back wheel support has a collar around its table base made of either polished marble or horn. The wheel has a lead band inserted around the circumference to increase its momentum. Something that appears to be a wheel finger is inserted into a hole in the table. If it is not a wheel finger (which would appear to be highly unnecessary) it may have supported a water cup in some manner.

HEIGHT: 24 in.
DEPTH: 16 in.
WIDTH: 13 in.

WHEEL NO. III

WHEEL NO. 112

This nineteenth century parlor wheel is probably from Germany.

The wheel, table and distaff are profusely decorated with ivory. Little wooden bells hang under the edge of the small, round table, the front side of which is flattened to accommodate the foot on the treadle. There is also a hole cut into the table which probably carried a water container for the spinning of flax. An interesting feature is the wooden flyer-axle and orifice. The only metal on the bobbin-flyer assembly is the guide hooks along the arms. The wheel uses a flyer drag. Very likely this was a trousseau wheel.

HEIGHT: 28.5 in.
DEPTH: 14.25 in.
WIDTH: 14 in.

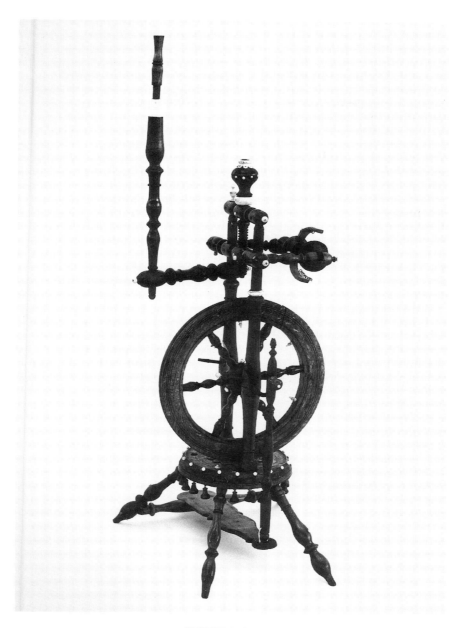

WHEEL NO. 112

WHEEL NO. 113

This is thought to be a trousseau wheel made in Germany or England during the nineteenth century.

On this wheel, as on wheels no. 113 and 115, the whole flyer, including the bobbin spindle and orifice, is made entirely of wood. Tension is adjusted by use of a flyer drag. The orifice is very large, suitable for wool spinning.

The wheel is dotted with ivory knobs and finials, as well as four ivory decorations on the table. The present "ivory" bells are replacements, the originals having been removed for some nefarious purpose, but the wire attachments from which they had been hung remained. Little leaf-shaped wooden overlays decorate the rim of the wheel. The distaff has a band of decorative pewter.

The distaff carrier is attached to the front wheel support. Another rod arises from the right side of the little round table and probably held a water vessel.

HEIGHT: 28 in.
DEPTH: 18 in.
WIDTH: 12.5 in.

WHEEL NO. 113

WHEEL NO. 114

This profusely decorated wheel most likely originated in Germany or England during the mid-nineteenth century.

Thirteen ivory bells hang from the underside of the heart-shaped table. Four more hang from the top of the distaff. Ivory and mother-of-pearl buttons decorate the tension screw, maidens, wheel rim and the edge of the table. In the middle of the rim, over the treadle, is an ivory rose. The finials on the wheel supports are tulip-shaped ivory and a large ivory tulip crowns the top of the distaff together with the four ivory bells. On the right of the table is a rod which undoubtedly carried a water vessel originally. Wheels like this were given as wedding presents or a part of a young woman's trousseau.

HEIGHT: 35.25 in. (without distaff)
            42 in. (with distaff)
DEPTH: 15 in.
WIDTH: 15.5 in.

WHEEL NO. 114

WHEEL NO. 115

This wheel was probably made in Germany in the nineteenth century. Heavily decorated, it is most truly a "parlor wheel." The rim of the wheel has very nice wood inlay. Between the spokes are prominent, gracefully shaped ivory spikes. Around the circumference of the table and on the footman are ivory buttons. On the top of the table is an ivory plate with a name and address on it. Unfortunately it is indecipherable now, although the word "Stadt" is still clear. This may have been the name of the maker or the owner.

HEIGHT: 26 in.
DEPTH: 18 in.
WIDTH: 12 in.

WHEEL NO. 115

WHEEL NO. 116

Patricia Baines (*Spinning Wheels, Spinners and Spinning*) places this wheel as made in York about 1790. It is a dainty wheel of exquisite workmanship.

On the table, inside the little railing, painted in deep pink, coral, white, purple, and soft green, are sprigs of roses, pansies, lilies, carnations, and leaves. The table is bordered by a leafy vine. The wheel supports are made of boxwood.

The whorl is missing; otherwise the wheel is in excellent condition. The quality of the flax remaining on the bobbin shows the wheel was used by no dilettante.

HEIGHT:	37.5 in.
DEPTH:	16 in.
WIDTH:	16 in.

WHEEL NO. 116

WHEEL NO. 117

This small French wheel was brought to New England from a village in the province of Alsace.

It is a very dainty wheel with fussy, delicate turnings. The wheel supports arise from the two horizontal bars. The tensioning device passes through the rod connecting the horizontal bars and the mother-of-all. A frame of three turned rods carries four turned spills that hold the horizontal bars. The orifice is small and suitable only for spinning flax. Across the front of the frame the treadle bar is attached by spikes. The treadle is bolted into this treadle bar. The treadle and orifice show much wear.

HEIGHT: 24 in.
DEPTH: 13.5 in.
LENGTH: 25.5 in.

WHEEL NO. 117

WHEEL NO. 118

This small wheel with a triangular base was made in France in the Normandy area probably in the late eighteenth century. The orifice is very small and the wheel undoubtedly was used for flax spinning.

All the finials and turnings are fine, elaborate without being fussy. The treadle is hinged to the front of the base by a metal bar which passes through the treadle into two pegs. There is no aperture on the frame to hold a distaff. However, at the extreme right hand side of the upper horizontal rod is a very small round hole which may have held a water cup.

HEIGHT: 28 in.
DEPTH: 15.5 in.
LENGTH: 29.5 in.

WHEEL NO. 118

WHEEL NO. 119

This late 18th or early 19th century wheel was made in France.

Its outstanding features are its rectangular base (see wheels 117 and 118), and its basket weave, lozenge-shaped distaff. The turnings and over-all lines are distinctive and charming.

HEIGHT: 23.5 in.
DEPTH: 13.5 in.
LENGTH: 27 in.

WHEEL NO. 119

WHEEL NO. 120

This wheel probably was made in Czechoslovakia or one of the Balkan states during the early nineteenth century. It has been suggested that is was a gypsy's wheel. Certainly it looks like the illustration of a fairy story.

The wood is very dark. There is a six-inch cut out of the table to accommodate the wheel. The table and wheel rim show the remains of profusely painted small beautiful flowers. The legs, maidens, mother-of-all, and distaff show the remains of stripes. Red, yellow, white, and almost purple were the predominant colors. The treadle board has a hole in each end through which the legs of the wheel are inserted and the board pushed up on the legs. The two boards that comprise the treadle are grooved along their edges for decoration. It shows much use and wear. There is only one place for a distaff carrier. The orifice is large, suitable for spinning wool, although there is old flax still on the bobbin. This is a romantic wheel that stirs the imagination.

HEIGHT:	33 in. (without distaff)
	65 in. (with distaff)
DEPTH:	14.5 in.
LENGTH:	30 in.

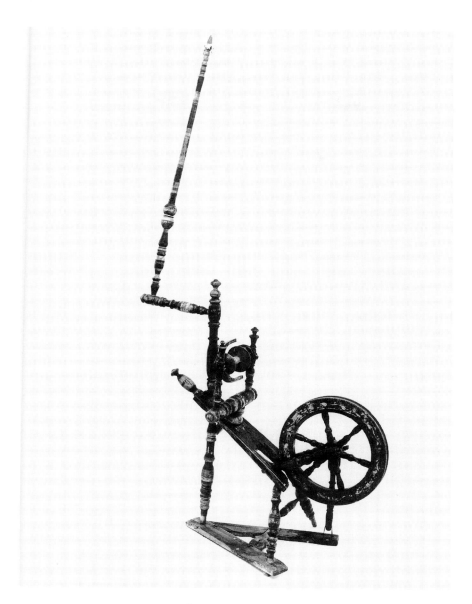

WHEEL NO. 120

WHEEL NO. 121

This wheel is thought to have originated in the Low Countries around the beginning of the nineteenth century. It is either a large parlor wheel or a small horizontal wheel. It is beautifully made and in excellent shape. The distaff carrier is unusual in that it has a hole in it to carry a water vessel. Usually the place for a water vessel came from the table.

HEIGHT: 30 in.
DEPTH: 15.5 in.
LENGTH: 31.5 in.

WHEEL NO. 121

WHEEL NO. 122

The outstanding features of this small wheel from England are the steep slope of its table and its beautiful turnings. The orifice is small and the wheel was made for spinning flax, probably in the second half of the nineteenth century. The cup is turned from a single piece of wood. There is no way of attaching the cup to the wheel, but the woods match and it was obviously made for this wheel. When purchased at auction in Massachusetts, the cup was tied to the wheel. It is very rare indeed to find a surviving cup although so many wheels had them originally.

HEIGHT: 29.75 in.
DEPTH: 17 in.
LENGTH: 31 in.

WHEEL NO. 122

WHEEL NO. 123

Like wheel no. 121, this wheel can be considered a parlor wheel or a small horizontal wheel. It is thought to be European made in the mid to late nineteenth century.

There are ivory tips to the finials and ivory buttons at each end of the mother-of-all. The treadle is attached to the treadle bar by leather strips. Its shape is unusual. The bracing of the three legs between the table and the treadle is rare (and much appreciated by anyone who has moved antique wheels often).

HEIGHT: 35 in.
DEPTH: 15 in.
LENGTH: 31 in.

WHEEL NO. 123

WHEEL NO. 124

This wheel is thought to be European, made in the early to mid nineteenth century.

The turnings are simple and the lines clear and pleasing. Its outstanding feature is the shape of the flyer. Instead of the customary single unit flyer with curved arms, this has a wooden disk into which are inserted two straight wooden arms.

HEIGHT: 29 in.
DEPTH: 18 in.
LENGTH: 38 in.

WHEEL NO. 124

WHEEL NO. 125

This is another small wheel thought to have come from the Balkan states.

The flyer assembly is enormous but original and typical of many of these little wheels from this area. The orifice is large for spinning wool. As on wheel no. 120, the table is cut to accommodate the wheel and the treadle board is attached by the table legs protruding through its two holes. The treadle is attached to the treadle board by leather straps. Red, blue, and green stripes are painted on the legs, mother-of-all tensioner, and wheel rim. The paint on this wheel appears to be old but not as old as the wheel. There are two holes on the table, one for the distaff carrier and the other for a water vessel.

In the early 1980s many of these wheels were imported into New England for the antique trade.

HEIGHT: 24 in.
DEPTH: 15 in.
LENGTH: 29 in.

WHEEL NO. 125

WHEEL NO. 126

This little wheel is thought to be from northern Europe or England, made in the early nineteenth century.

It has an unusually steeply sloped table and the maidens are exceptionally long, raising the height of the orifice to twenty-seven inches. The wheel supports have no braces but are stable, protruding as they do far below the table. The legs are very spraddled to give the spinning wheel more stability.

HEIGHT: 30 in.
DEPTH: 22.5 in.
LENGTH: 30 in.

WHEEL NO. 126

WHEEL NO. 127

This very small wheel is thought to have originated in England or northern Europe in the late eighteenth or early nineteenth century.

Instead of the table being cut away to accommodate the wheel, it is very steeply sloped. As usual with these small wheels, the flyer assembly is very large. The orifice is large enough for spinning thick wool. The turnings on the legs and wheel supports are elaborate and pleasing. There are two holes in the table for the distaff carrier and a water vessel.

HEIGHT: 23.5 in.
DEPTH: 15 in.
LENGTH: 26 in.

WHEEL NO. 127

WHEEL NO. 128

This very small ebonized wheel is probably from the Balkans, made around the beginning of the nineteenth century. The large orifice on the flyer suggests it was made for spinning wool as well as flax. There are two holes in the table to hold a distaff carrier and a water container. There is the remnant of some sort of decoration on the table, possibly a carved wooden rose, which has broken off.

HEIGHT: 22 in.
DEPTH: 13 in.
LENGTH: 25.5 in

WHEEL NO. 128

Accessory Tools

ACCESSORY I

These spindles are thought to have come from eastern Europe except for the extreme right hand one which is from Guatemala and is probably modern. It is unreal to attempt to date the others.

Their length varies from 14 to 25 inches, and their weight from 3.5 to 4.5 ounces.

The extreme left spindle has either hemp or tow on it. The right hand Guatemalan one has brown cotton.

The two spindles adjacent to the Guatemalan one have remnants of red and green painted rings.

ACCESSORY I

ACCESSORY 2

This spindle rack came from Bulgaria. It has places for 13 spindles; eight came with it, and of these five appear to be a matched set. They vary in length from 16 to 17 inches, and in weight from 1.25 to 1.75 ounces. Five have similar carvings and appear to have been made of the same type of wood.

The other three spindles very in length, being 10.25, 13.5, and 15 inches long. The smallest weighs just over half an ounce.

ACCESSORY 2

ACCESSORY 3

These distaffs were used to hold the prepared flax, and at times wool, which the spinner was spinning. They appear to be from the eighteenth and nineteenth century and, except where noted, probably come from eastern Europe. They were pushed into the ground or inserted in a pot of soil or small stones beside the spinner.

No. 4 has a flat instead of a round stem. It would have been stuck under the belt of the spinner allowing her (or him) to spin on the drop spindle while walking, minding the flock, or standing talking with the neighbors.

No. 5 has a dove painted in the top circle, a young woman's head in the second circle, and the head of a man and a woman in the third circle. It is thought that this was an engagement present.

No. 7 comes from Spain. In Ste. Teresa of Avila's cell in the Carmelite convent at Beas is a similarly-shaped distaff.

No. 6, with its short stem, probably belongs to a spinning wheel and has been mislaid.

No.8 is known to have come from Greece. It and no. 5 both have a large wooden hook behind the decorated top which holds the flax.

No. 2 is painted a dark green.

Nos. 1, 2, and 6 have decorative lines cut or traced on them.

LENGTH: Longest 48 in.
              Shortest 24 in.

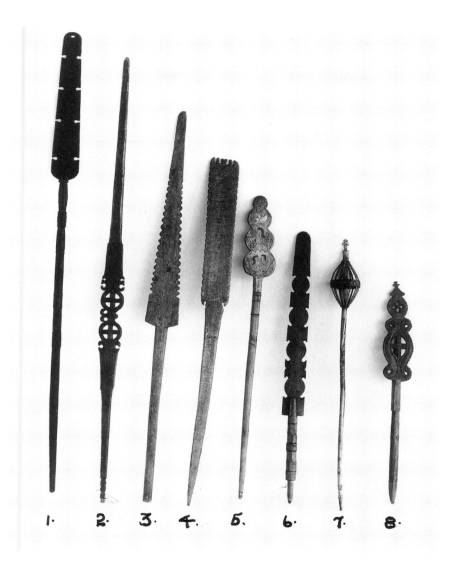

ACCESSORY 3

QUILLERS

Quillers were used to wind the bobbins for the weaving shuttles. Often these bobbins were the ends of goose quills, hence the name "quiller."

The most usual form was a table and wheel, similar to the spindle spinning wheel, only a little smaller. In place of the post and spindle there was a box across which was affixed a removable metal bar with a whorl. The quill slipped onto the metal bar and the drive band passed around the whorl and the wheel. Extra quills and the ball of yarn from which the quills were to be filled were placed in the box.

There is great variation in the size of the quill some quillers can accommodate. Large quills were undoubtedly needed for weaving very thick spun wool or rags for rug weaving.

The following pages show a variety of types of quillers.

ACCESSORY 4

This quiller came from New Hampshire. Although quite primitively finished, it is a carefully made piece of equipment. The whorl end of the spindle fits into a hole in the left hand post, and the other end slides easily into a slot in the right hand one. A pivoted peg secures this end firmly.

ACCESSORY 4

ACCESSORY 5

This is the most common quiller found in New England, probably built in the late eighteenth or early nineteenth century.

The spindle, fitted with a whorl, fits into holes on each side of the box. As before, the box holds the ball of yarn and the filled and unfilled bobbins.

HEIGHT: 31.25
DEPTH: 15 in.
LENGTH: 31 in.

ACCESSORY 5

ACCESSORY 6

This is another New England quiller, larger than Accessory 5, otherwise basically the same. This wheel has no handle for turning it. Possibly it was with tools such as this that "wheel fingers" were most useful.

HEIGHT: 41 in.
DEPTH: 15.5 in.
LENGTH: 45 in.

ACCESSORY 6

ACCESSORY 7

This quiller came from Canada.

The tensioning mechanism is the same as the traditional tensioner used on treadle spinning wheels. This is accomplished by a block fitted into a slit in the table and protruding into the box where it is secured. The screw handle passes through the end of the table into the block. There are unused holes in each side of the box which are in line with an unused hole in the block. They suggest a mistake was made in understanding the placement of the tensioning mechanism. Another hole made in the front end of the box remains unexplained.

The wheel is turned by the handle on the spoke

HEIGHT: 39.25 in.
DEPTH: 19 in.
LENGTH: 48 in.

ACCESSORY 7

ACCESSORY 8

This is an American quiller. The bat head is unusual in shape, size, and function. On one spoke there is a wooden handle to facilitate turning the wheel. There is no tensioning mechanism.

HEIGHT: 39.5 in.
DEPTH: 17.5 in.
LENGTH: 44 in.

ACCESSORY 8

ACCESSORY 9

This seems to be a treadled quiller with a missing footman.

There are two large wooden pegs to hold the quiller bar, the front one of which is a cube measuring one and a quarter inches. The bar across the top of the maidens seems to have no purpose other than to stabilize the maidens. It shows no evidence of having been used as a brake.

There is no tensioning mechanism. The braces of the wheel posts are in front of the wheel instead of behind in the customary manner. The wheel has one groove in the rim. There is a slot in the protuberance of the table the function of which is not known.

The wheel is from the late eighteenth or very early nineteenth century. Purchased in New Hampshire, it is thought to be either New England or Canadian origin.

HEIGHT: 40.5 in.
DEPTH: 12 in.
LENGTH: 37 in.

ACCESSORY 9

ACCESSORY 10

This is a large, cumbersome, primitive quiller purchased in Pennsylvania. It was probably made in the late eighteenth or early nineteenth century.

HEIGHT: 32.5 in.
DEPTH: 29.5 in.
LENGTH: 26.5 in.

ACCESSORY 10

ACCESSORY II

This unusual quiller was purchased in Massachusetts. Its origin is unknown but it was probably made in the middle of the nineteenth century when accelerating wheels were becoming popular on spinning wheels. It functions in the same manner as the preceding quillers.

HEIGHT: 33.3 in.
DEPTH: 24.5 in.
LENGTH: 31 in.

ACCESSORY II

REELS

When the spindle or bobbin is filled with spun and plied yarn, the thread must be put into skeins to be washed and dyed. This is accomplished by the reel.

Reels vary from primitive, four-armed structures that can be pivoted on a stand to beautiful drawing-room pieces of furniture. Small reels made entirely of ivory are sometimes seen. These were usually used for skeining silk or wool embroidery threads. In Canada a "wrap reel" was common. These consist of four arms mounted on a post which fits into a rectangular frame on the floor.

On most reels the crosspiece at the end of the arms has a lip at each end, except for one end of one crosspiece. This crosspiece is known as "the stranger." The lips prevent the yarn from sliding off the reel as it is being wound on; the stranger allows the spinner to remove the skein when it is finished. Some reels, instead of having a missing lip, have one arm pegged. By removing the peg, the crosspiece folds back and the skein can be removed.

Some reels are only turned and it is up to the spinner to count the rotations and thus know the yardage in the skein. Many reels have a mechanism known as "the clicker". With these reels, the spinner starts winding the yarn onto the reel when she has turned it until a thin piece of wood has clicked against the counting gear. She continues to turn until the next click. On most American reels the distance between clicks measures about 85 yards. This gives a skein of 80 yards, allowing for shrinkage in washing. More elaborate reels have a pointer which turns with the reel. These are known as "clock reels." They have the advantage over the click reels of letting the spinner know approximately how much yardage she has, if she has not a full skein.

Examples of these reels may be seen on the following pages.

ACCESSORY 12

ACCESSORY 12

Who can resist, when looking at these weird shaped objects, chanting
    "Niddy - noddy; Niddy - noddy,
Two heads, one body!"
    They are simple primitive tools for making skeins of the spun yarn from the spinning wheel bobbin.
    The large one takes up 2 yards, seven inches, with each complete turn around the four arms. The small one, probably used for finer silk or wool embroidery thread, or linen or cotton sewing thread, takes up 1 yard 7 in. each full turn. On both, three arms end in a raised lip to stop the thread from sliding off. The fourth arm is smooth to allow the skein to be removed when completed.
    As the spinner wound the yarn on, she usually counted the completed turns by this chant:
    "One, 'taint one, 'twill be one, 'tis one;
    Two, 'taint two, 'twill be two, 'tis two;" etc.
saying one phrase as she passed each arm. Knowing it was two yards around (plus extra for shrinkage) she thus had a good idea of her yardage when finished winding.

ACCESSORY 13

These are "wrap" reels. The one on the left came to New Hampshire from Portugal; the one on the right is Canadian from the province of Quebec. On both the bar holding the arms lifts out of the frame, allowing the skein to be slipped off.

The Quebec reel was also used when plying. One bobbin would be wound off onto one end of the reel, another onto the other end, then both ends together could be fed back into the wheel for plying. This system made it unnecessary to have several bobbins for each wheel and saved the time changing bobbins.

Left Reel
HEIGHT: 26 in.
DEPTH: 24.5 in.
WIDTH: 24 in.
Length of yarn for one turn; 63.5 in.

Right Reel
HEIGHT: 25 in.
DEPTH: 26.25 in.
WIDTH: 21.5 in.
Length of yarn for one turn; 52 in.

ACCESSORY 13

ACCESSORY 14

It is unknown where this reel originated. It is well made but the finish is primitive. Instead of having a stranger, one arm is hinged; by removal of a wooden peg this arm folds back allowing the skein to be removed. Like the two preceding reels, the bar holding the arms lifts out of the frame.

HEIGHT: 39 in.
DEPTH: 18 in.
WIDTH: 27.5 in.
Yardage of one round: 2 yds 2.5 in.

ACCESSORY 14

ACCESSORY 15

This reel came from Massachusetts and two like it have been seen since it was purchased. This suggests that it was a very popular design when made, probably in the mid nineteenth century. It is well made, slightly smaller than many reels and equipped with a simple clock which measures the yardage. Its interesting feature is that the main post enters the table at an angle so that it slopes backwards. This is most convenient to the spinner, for it allows her to see the yardage easily, while it is in use, without bending over or getting up from her chair.

HEIGHT: 37.5 in.
DEPTH: 12.5 in.
WIDTH: 24 in.
Yardage on one round: 2 yds. 2 in.
No. of turns between "clicks": 40

ACCESSORY 15

ACCESSORY 16

This four armed reel is interesting because its mechanism is horizontal rather than the more usual vertical type.

It is equipped with a "clicker" but no clock. Unfortunately the worn gear is slightly broken which makes it impossible to measure the number of revolutions between clicks.

This reel has no lips on the arms to prevent the thread from slipping off.

HEIGHT: 35.25 in.
DEPTH: 25 in.
LENGTH: 26.5 in.
Yardage on one round: 2 yds. 2 in.

ACCESSORY 16

ACCESSORY 17

This reel was probably made in the late eighteenth or early nineteenth century and is typical of those used in New England farm houses. It is equipped with a clock and still works as smoothly as the day it was made.

HEIGHT: 39 in.
DEPTH: 24 in.
WIDTH: 25 in.
Yardage on one round: 2 yds. 2.5 in.
No. of turns between clicks: 40

ACCESSORY 17

ACCESSORY 18

This reel is a beautiful, very Victorian, piece of drawing room furniture. It has a clicker but no clock.

There is no stranger and when first seen there appears no possible way of removing the skein. The secret is that, on one arm, the top bulgy turned piece is actually a sleeve. When it is pushed up, the pivoted arm underneath folds back on itself, allowing removal of the skein.

Another unusual and interesting feature is a peg inserted into the lower support of the frame, which locks the reel in position so that the reel may not be turned without first removing the peg.

HEIGHT: 37.5 in.
DEPTH: 16.7 in.
WIDTH: 32 in.
Yardage on one round: 2 yds. 20 in.
One missing tooth on the gear prevents
counting the number of turns between clicks.

ACCESSORY 18

ACCESSORY 19

This is another reel with a clicker but no clock, showing a rather more sophisticated mechanism.

HEIGHT: 37 in.
DEPTH: 19.5 in.
WIDTH: 25 in.
Yardage on one round: 2 yds. 3 in.
No. of turns between clicks: 40

ACCESSORY 19

ACCESSORY 20

This wrap reel is thought to have come from Switzerland. The wood, the tooling and the workmanship are very reminiscent of wheel no. 52.

The purpose of the holes along the base is not clear, unless it was used to wind many separate skeins of linen, perhaps from a small parlor wheel. It has a nice touch of whimsey in the clock indicator shaped like a mouse.

HEIGHT: 28.5 in.
DEPTH: 23.5 in.
WIDTH: 24 in.
Yardage on one round: 2 yds.
Clock mechanism not working

ACCESSORY 2O

ACCESSORY 21

This is another drawing room reel, beautifully made and finished.

Here the clock face is covered with glass and the face is painted with small flowers and vines, also the date 182? (the last figure is too faded to read.) It is believed to have come from Connecticut or Massachusetts.

HEIGHT: 43 in.
DEPTH: 16.5 in.
WIDTH: 24.25 in.
Yardage on one round: 2 yds 3 in.
No. of turns between clicks: 40

ACCESSORY 2I

ACCESSORY 22

This small reel is unique in its utter simplicity. A 14-inch piece of wood, tapered at each end, is slotted at right angles into another identical piece. At the end of each arm is a five inch bar. These bars have a lip at each end except for one, which is the "stranger." On this arm is a handle. The arms are mounted on a two inch cylinder which in the back is cut down to a three quarter inch stem. The stem slips into a hole in the upright support, thus allowing the arms to pivot when they are turned by the handle. The operator counts the number of turns executed to calculate the yardage wound on.

HEIGHT: 17.5 in.
DEPTH: 7.75 in.
WIDTH: 13.75 in.
Yardage on one round: 1 yd., 6 in

ACCESSORY 22

ACCESSORY 23

This tool, made entirely of metal, is both a reel and a swift. When used as a reel, the arms are extended to their full length and the wing nut tightened. There is a clicker counting mechanism. The extended arms take up two yards, two and a half inches with each revolution. The counter clicks at every forty turns.

When used as a swift, the arms are loosened and pushed toward each other to the position needed to hold the shrunken skein taut.

The tool could also be used as a blocker for stretching and drying washed skeins.

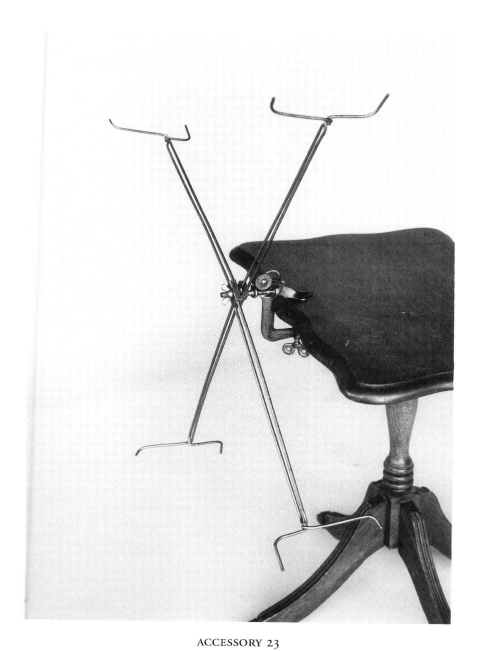

ACCESSORY 23

ACCESSORY 24

This click reel came from Prince Edward Island, Canada. Probably made in the early nineteenth century, it had belonged to only one family where it received much use. The family, even in the first quarter of the twentieth century, spun and wove their own cloth. The reel is still in perfect working order.

Each single turn takes up 79 inches, and the clicker clicks every 100 turns.

HEIGHT: 40 in.
DEPTH: 14.5 in.
WIDTH: 26.5 in.

ACCESSORY 24

SWIFTS

Swifts are used to hold the skeins taut while the yarn is rolled into balls for knitting or weaving. Shrinkage has taken place during the washing, dyeing, drying process making the skeins of somewhat variable lengths. Therefore the swift must be adjustable to hold the individual skein fully extended.

The following pages show a variety of swifts with different methods of adjusting to the skein length.

ACCESSORY 25

This is the simplest of all swifts. The base is a solid heavy tree butt, probably oak, reinforced by an iron band to prevent splitting. The frame bearing four sloped arms is inserted into the centre of the base where it can rotate easily. There are no movable or removable parts on the arms. The size of the skein is accommodated by simply pushing it down the frame until it is taut. This swift could also be used as a skein blocker.

HEIGHT: 39 in.
WIDTH: 21.25 in.

ACCESSORY 25

ACCESSORY 26

The base of this swift is a split log from the centre of which arises a post. Two arms at right angles to each other rotate on this post. Each arm has three holes, 1.5 inches apart and the arm peg may be placed in any one of these holes. This allows this swift to accommodate a skein of 66 inches down to 42 inches.

HEIGHT: 28.5 in.
WIDTH: 18.25 in.

ACCESSORY 26

ACCESSORY 27

The base of this swift is a planed board from which arises a vertical slotted board. The axle of the turning frame fits into the notches of this vertical board. Each arm has three sets of holes and a wooden pin can be inserted into whichever set is required to hold the skein taut. This swift accommodates skeins from 66 inches down to 54 inches.

HEIGHT: 38.5 in.
DEPTH: 25.5 in.
WIDTH: 7.25 in.

ACCESSORY 27

ACCESSORY 28

This swift shows yet another way of holding the washed skein. The base consists of two pleasantly shaped and fitted pieces of wood. The stem arises from the centre of these crossed pieces and ends in a long dowel onto which fits the frame. Each arm has a fixed dowel towards the stem, then another movable outer arm which can be placed in the most exterior hole or in one of the holes placed 2 inches apart along the arm. Skeins from 60 inches to 40 inches can be held taut.

HEIGHT: 41.25
DEPTH: 22 in.

ACCESSORY 28

ACCESSORY 29

This rather dumpy swift has a comfortable appealing appearance. While not exactly a "drawing room" piece, it has nicely turned arms and the base is well finished and shaped. The outer dowels can be moved from the outer position three inches on each arm. A skein of 67 inches down to 55 inches can be held taut.

HEIGHT: 29 in.
DEPTH: 25 in.

ACCESSORY 29

ACCESSORY 30

This is probably the most popular swift of the nineteenth century. It is commonly referred to as an umbrella swift because of its opening method. The lower bulb is pushed up the stem to the desired position and secured in place by a peg which slips into a hole in the center rod. Over a length of six and three quarters inches, the center rod has a hole every half inch.

When the arms are extended to maximum position, one revolution takes up two yards and nine inches with each revolution.

The table has beading along the front and back edges and chip carving along each side.

On the top is the cup to hold a partially wound ball.

HEIGHT: 32 in.
DEPTH: 9.5 in.
WIDTH: 11.5 in.

ACCESSORY 30

ACCESSORY 31

This beautiful little swift was probably used for skeining sewing thread or embroidery silk or wool. Unlike most umbrella swifts, the arms are extended by pushing the top bulb down instead of the lower bulb up. The bulb can be stopped anywhere along the stem, thus varying the length of the skein. When the arms are fully extended, one revolution takes up two yards and four inches of thread.

At the top is the cup to hold the partially wound ball if it has to be put down. The clamp is made entirely of wood.

ACCESSORY 31

ACCESSORY 32

This is a metal swift made to clamp onto a table.

When the wing nut is loosened, the arms slide toward each other. The skein is slipped on and the arms are pulled in opposite directions until the skein is taut, then the wing nut is tightened. The arms revolve on the pin of the clamp.

When the arms are fully extended, one revolution carries two yards of thread.

HEIGHT: 50 in.
DEPTH: 24 in.
LENGTH: 22.5 in.

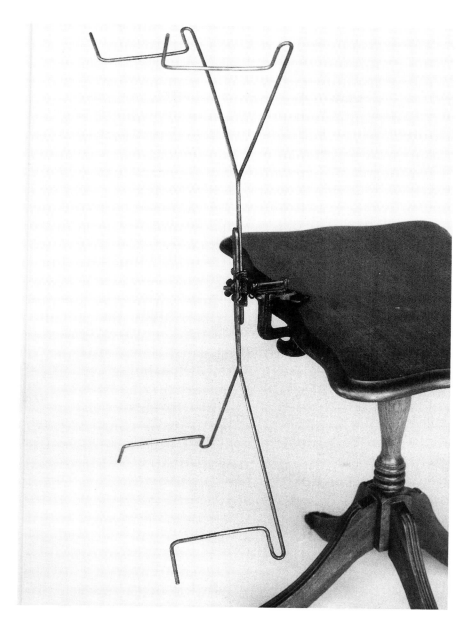

ACCESSORY 32

ACCESSORY 33 AND 33A

These two small umbrella table swifts are probably from the nineteenth century. The one on the left is made of brass, the one on the right of wood. On both, the bottom is pushed up the stem to open the swift. A small brass screw secures the position on the left hand swift; a wooden peg inserted through any one of many holes in the stem secures the right hand one. The left swift accommodates up to a 44-inch skein, the right up to a 56-inch skein.

Left Swift		*Right Hand Swift*	
HEIGHT:	13.5 in.	HEIGHT:	18.75 in.
WIDTH:	18 in. (extended)	WIDTH:	20 in. (extended)

ACCESSORY 33 AND 33A

ACCESSORY 34

This is known as a squirrel cage swift. It serves as a swift but its greatest use was as a yarn blocker. The wet skeins are put over the cages and they are stretched by separating the cages as far apart as possible. As the skeins dry, moisture naturally runs down to the bottom. By rolling the cages, the wet bottom of the skein is brought up to the top and the very wet wool starts drying. This makes the drying of the skeins quicker and evener. This swift can accommodate up to a 72-inch skein.

HEIGHT: 40.25 in.
DEPTH: 12 in.
WIDTH: 19.5 in.

ACCESSORY 34

ACCESSORY 35

These table-clamp swifts offer an interesting contrast to each other.

The one on the left is an elegant, carefully made, fruit-wood swift for use in a drawing room. These adjustable arms are secured in place by the wood clamp above them which ends in a cup to hold the ball of thread. Sitting in the cup is a wood ball with a bored out stem; when lifted, its underside is a red velvet pincushion. The whole swift can be lifted off the table clamp and the pin cushion fitted on to the clamp spike that held the swift.

This swift was probably made in the Victorian era. It is thought to have been used for netting. The required amount of thread would be measured on the swift which would then be removed and replaced by the pincushion to which the primary thread of the net would be anchored. Another possibility is that the swift was used for winding sewing thread from a skein, and the pincushion served as a "hemming bird."

The table swift on the right is a very forthright, home-made, crudely-finished piece. The upper arm support is raised or lowered and anchored into place by a peg passing through the centre column.

ACCESSORY 35

ACCESSORY 36

This is also a skein holder made to facilitate the changing of a skein into a ball. However, calling it a swift does not seem appropriate.

The two outer pieces with pegs at each end slide along grooves on the center piece of wood. These can be secured wherever desired by tightening the wooden screws which pass through them and press against the center board. A wooden table clamp, equipped with a short metal spike which fits into a center hole on the center board, allows the holder to be mounted on a table.

This is a beautifully and simply made piece. It has been suggested that it is Shaker in origin; however, nothing is known to confirm this.

LENGTH: closed — 13.5 in.
            maximum extension — 32 in.

ACCESSORY 36

ACCESSORY 37

Before the fleece can be carded for spinning, the fibres must be pulled apart and bits of foreign material removed. This is known as "picking." It is a somewhat slow and tedious occupation, usually done by hand.

This apparatus, made in Grenoble, France, in the nineteenth century, greatly speeds up the process. It consists of a wooden bench at one end of which sits the operator. At the other end, within the open box, is a curved sheet of metal bearing close-set, 1.5 inches long, sharp spikes. At the lowest point of the curved metal, a piece of wire mesh replaces the spikes. This allows chaff and foreign matter to fall through the apparatus as it is freed from the fleece. A piece of similarly spiked metal, curved to fit the contours of the lower piece, hangs from the superstructure. The slits in the structure's arms allow the height of the upper piece to be adjusted carefully so that it just meets the lower spikes. Fleece is fed into the area where the top and bottom spiked pieces meet. The operator swings the upper piece back and forth. The spikes, as they meet, tease the fleece apart and toss it beyond the machine. In this state it is ready to be carded.

This machine bears the name "Pratt and Blanc," followed by a number assumed to be the patent number, then underneath "Grenoble," the place of origin. This information is printed on the wooden bench, and on the metal superstructure. Several picking machines from France have been seen in New England but there is no evidence that they were ever made in this country.

HEIGHT: 29 in.
DEPTH: 15 in.
LENGTH: 44 in.

ACCESSORY 37

ACCESSORY 38

After picking, the fleece must be either carded or combed. Carding is done usually with hand carders similar to those shown on the left. They consist of two boards, sometimes flat, sometimes slightly curved, with a firm handle on each. The boards are covered on one side with "carding cloth", a canvas holding close-set wire pins. A small amount of fleece is spread on one carder and the second one is drawn several times, gently over it. The fibres are thus straightened and laid parallel to each other. When in order, the fibres are then rolled up into a rolag. Spinning is carried out across the fibres, making a soft, light yarn which holds much air and is therefore very warm, but not windproof. Cotton is carded in the same way using a very fine carding cloth.

LENGTH: 9.5 in.
WIDTH: 4.5 in.

ACCESSORY 38

ACCESSORY 39

These wool combs were used for preparing fleece to be spun along the length of the fibre into worsted yarn.

The combs consist of heavy wooden handles with six-inch cross bars reinforced with metal. Into these cross bars are inserted three or four rows of sturdy, sharp metal spikes about eight inches long.

One comb, loaded with fleece would be clamped firmly to the bench. The comber then repeatedly pulled the other comb through the loaded fleece, pulling out and discarding the short hairs and lining up the long hairs in parallel. Alternating combs, this procedure would be done over and over until a bat of perfect long fibres was produced. The bats were then drawn out into a continuous roving.

Because of the weight of the combs, men were usually employed as combers. Preparation of the fleece for spinning is of primary importance, and the men who were combers were considered the top artisans of the spinning industry.

ACCESSORY 39

ACCESSORY 40

This is a carding bench. One carder is mounted on the elevated end of the bench where it fits into grooves. The operator, seated on the other end of the bench, draws the second carder through the fleece placed on the mounted carder. The carders on these benches are nearly double the size of the hand carders, so the work proceeds at a greater pace.

This carding bench came from New Hampshire. An identical pair of carders (without the bench) are in the collection, which suggests it was not an uncommon tool. It is thought to have come from the late eighteenth or early nineteenth century.

HEIGHT: 29.5 in.
DEPTH: 20 in.
LENGTH: 35.5 in.

ACCESSORY 40

ACCESSORY 41

The following five tools are all used in the preparation of flax for spinning linen thread:

Accessory 41 is a flax break. After the flax has been dried, wetted, and dried again, the outer hard sheath of the stem must be removed from the inner fibres. To accomplish this, the flax stems are beaten to break the outer cover into small fragments.

Some flax breaks have two beaters, some have only one. The flax is drawn across the bar and (with this breaker) the two beaters are raised and smashed down on the stems as they pass along.

In many parts of the world instead of the flax break, a flax mallet is used to break the sheath. The stems are simply hammered against a hard surface. Such an implement is shown in the next photograph.

HEIGHT: 29.25 in.
DEPTH: 20 in.
LENGTH: 35.5 in.

ACCESSORY 41

ACCESSORY 42

SCUTCHING KNIVES

After the outer sheath of the flax has been thoroughly broken, the pieces must be removed from the fine inner fibres. This is accomplished by passing a scutching knife along the fibres and scraping the little pieces away. The first two scutching knives come from Europe, the second two from New England.

Below the scutching knives is a European Flax mallet.

Scutching Knives	1	2	3	4
LENGTH:	19 in.	16 in.	23.7 in.	26.7 in.
WIDTH:	45 in.	4 in.	2.5 in.	2.5 in.

Mallet
LENGTH: 13.5 in.
CIRCUMFERENCE: 12.2 in.

ACCESSORY 42

ACCESSORY 43

FLAX HACKLES

After removing the outer sheath with the scutching knife, the flax fibres are passed through the hackle. This consists of a block of wood which holds metal, seven inch long, sharp spikes in staggered rows half an inch apart. The fibres are combed through these spikes until any remaining pieces of debris or broken threads are removed. Usually several hackles varying from coarse to fine were used. When not in use, the hackles were usually kept covered by a fitted wooden box.

OVERALL LENGTH:	21.7 in.	SPIKED AREA LENGTH:	7.2 in.
OVERALL WIDTH:	5.5 in.	SPIKED AREA LENGTH:	3.7 in.
OVERALL HEIGHT:	7 in.	SPIKED AREA LENGTH:	5.3 in.

ACCESSORY 43

ACCESSORY 44

This flax hackle is either from Russia or made in the Russian tradition. Purchased in New England, it reputedly came from a Doukhobor community in British Columbia.

In its present state it has one hackle, all wood, carved into fine teeth from a single board. A place for a second hackle is at the other end of the bench. It undoubtedly was either coarser or finer than the existing one. This is a beautiful piece of workmanship with lovely lines.

LENGTH: 33.7 in.
DEPTH: 10.75 in.
HEIGHT: 38.5 in.

ACCESSORY 44

ACCESSORY 45

This hackle bench is from New England. The operator sat in the middle and on one side had a coarse hackle and on the other a fine. The bench is made of an extraordinarily hard wood.

Bench		*Spiked Blocks*	
HEIGHT:	25.5	HEIGHT:	6.5 in.
DEPTH:	23 in.	DEPTH:	2.75 in.
LENGTH:	64 in.	LENGTH:	3.2 in.

ACCESSORY 45

ACCESSORY 46

This photograph is of a freestanding distaff. Only one other has been seen over the years these wheels and accessories have been collected. It was a carved and beautifully finished article.

This distaff, standing about four feet high, is very simple with no decoration but carefully made. It is thought to be American, most likely New England in origin.

ACCESSORY 46

ACCESSORY 47

This apparatus has been named a straw press, a flax break, and a cotton gin.

The machine works in the same manner as the mangle of an old fashioned washing machine; the pressure between the rollers is adjustable.

When wet rye straw was braided for making straw hats and bags, the braids needed flattening. This seems the most likely function of this tool.

However, it has been used satisfactorily as a flax break. It makes much lighter work than using a break such as accessory 42, although for a large quantity it would be slower.

In a museum in South Carolina there is a similar tool labeled a cotton gin. Supposedly the pressure between the rollers extruded the seed as the cotton bolle was passed through.

HEIGHT: 27 in.
DEPTH: 20 in.
LENGTH: 21 in.

ACCESSORY 47

ACCESSORY 48

This overstuffed spinner's chair was found at an auction in Hillsborough, New Hampshire. The upholstery was worn out and the stuffing exuberantly spilling. It has been restored.

The chair was made without a left arm to allow the spinner an unimpeded long left hand draw.

The seat is 15 inches high. The left corner of the seat is curved into the left side. The wood is probably cherry. There are decorative designs on the front of the right arm and along the front wood of the seat.

With the right arm placed on the padded arm rest, the firm but cushioned seat and the upholstered, almost vertical back, it is an exceedingly comfortable chair for sitting to spin.

HEIGHT: 34 in.
WIDTH: 22 in.
DEPTH: 27 in

ACCESSORY 48

Tables of Measurements

SPINDLE WHEELS (measurements in inches)

WHEEL NO.	WHEEL						TABLE				SPINDLE		LEGS	
	Circumference	No. of pieces in rim	Width of rim	No. of grooves in rim	No. of spokes	Height of axle	Length	Width	Slope	Thickness	Height	Length	Length front	Length back
1	45.5	3	5	0	10	30	91.5	9 > 12.5	5		14	broken	8.5	broken
2	17	n/a	n/a	n/a	8	13.5	31	24	0	1.5	5	11.95	n/a	n/a
3	3.5	n/a	n/a	n/a	0	3.5	9	4	0	0.12	1.25	5.5	n/a	n/a
4	5.5/2.3	n/a	0.25	1	n/a	n/a	n/a	n/a	n/a	n/a	n/a	6	n/a	n/a
5	48	1	2.5	0	10	39.5	43	4.5 > 5.5	8.75	1.75	43.25	11.25	18	15.75
6	40.5	1	1.25	1	10	38.75	45.25	3 > 8.25	18.25	2.5	49.5	13.75	28	14.5
7	44.5	1	2	3	12	35.5	40.25	4.75	9.25	2.25	41.5	12	19.25	12.5
8	45.25	1	2.75	0	10	37.25	41.5	5 > 5.5	6.75	2	42.5	12	16	14.5
9	43.5	2	2.5	0	12	37	44	6	7	2	41	12	19.75	14.5
10	17	1	1.5	0	8	20	22	2.5 > 4.25	3.25	1.5	23.5	broken	12.5	8.75
11	33.5	1	2.5	0	10	13.25	38	5 < 4.25	4.5	3/2	29	14	14	11
12	45	2	2.75	0	10	38.25	41.5	6.5 < 4.75	10.5	2.25	41.5	11.75	17.5	14
13	40.5	1	2	1	10	41.25	51	6.75	2	2.5	47.75	12.75	16.5	13.25
14	43.5	2	2.5	0	12	34	42.5	5.75 > 6.2	13	1.75	42	15.75	19.5	10.5
15	45.5	3	2	0	10	38	40	6.5	9	2	41	12	16	14
16	39	1	2.5	0	8	38	44	6	0	2.25	43.75	14.5	16	16
17	45.25	1	2	1	12	35.5	42.5	6.75	8	2.25	44.5	12.5	19.75	12.25
18	44.5	2	2.5	0	10	38.5	45.5	5.5 > 6.5	8	2/2.7	45	11.5	17.5	15
19	47.75	1	2.5	0	12	38.5	41.5	6.5	7.8	2	39	12.75	18	14.5
20	46	1	2.5	0	12	38.5	49.5	8 < 5.7	5	2.25	41	11	16.25	12.75
21	24	n/a	1.5	0	10	36.5	······WHEEL DOES NOT FIT INTO THESE CLASSIFICATIONS······							
22	43.5		1.5	1	10	29	······WHEEL DOES NOT FIT INTO THESE CLASSIFICATIONS······							
23	45.5		1.5	1	12		······WHEEL DOES NOT FIT INTO THESE CLASSIFICATIONS······							
24	20.75	1	1.5	0	8	n/a	······WHEEL DOES NOT FIT INTO THESE CLASSIFICATIONS······							
25	9.75	1	0.37	0	6	n/a	······WHEEL DOES NOT FIT INTO THESE CLASSIFICATIONS······							
28	28	2	3	0	10	25.5	33	7.5/4.5	3.75	2	21.25	11	10.5	9

VERTICAL BOBBIN FLYER WHEELS (measurements in inches)

WHEEL NO.	WHEEL						BOBBIN-FLYER								TABLE				LEGS	
	Diameter	No. of pieces in rim	No. of grooves in rim	Width of rim	No. of spokes	Height of axle	Length	No. of grooves in whorl	Diameter of whorl groove	Diameter of bobbin groove	Distance above top of wheel	Distance to side of wheel	Size of orifice	Height of orifice	Height	Depth	Width	Shape	Number	Length
39	13.5	4	2	1.4	6	14.7	12.7	1	3.7	2.8	8	—	0.4	29.5	8	14	18	T	3	6.5
40	21	4	2	1.6	8	18.5	11	1	2.7	2.2	—	5.5r	0.5	30	7.5	13	16.5	T	3	6.5
41	13.5	4	2	1.2	6	17	9.6	1	2.4	2.1	7	—	0.4	30	9	8	13.5	T	3	9
42	18	4	2	1.6	8	17.5	10.2	2	2.6	2.2	7	—	0.5	34	8	12.5	16.5	Circ.	3	7
43	13.5	4	0	1.2	6	16	10	1	3.3	2.4	7.2	—	0.5	27.5	6.5	7.5	—	Octag.	3	8
44	21.2	4	0	2	10	19	9.5	1	2.6	1.8	2.2	—	0.5	34	7.2	8.2	8.2	T	3	8.5
45	15.5	4	2	1.4	6	16	10	1	2.6	2.4	6	—	0.4	29	6.5	10.5	16.7	T	3	5
46	15.2	4	0	1.5	8	19	11.5	1	2.6	2	7	8.6.5r	0.4	30.7	10	13.5	15.5	T	3	8
47	18.5	4	2	2	8	16	6.2	1	2.3	2		$6.5rt	0.4	28.5	n/a	n/a	n/a	n/a	n/a	n/a
48	21	4	0	1.2	8	12.5	10.5	n/a	n/a	2.7	7	8.6.5lt	0.5	27	n/a	n/a	n/a	n/a	n/a	n/a
49	19	4	0	1.2	8	11	11.5	n/a	n/a	2.7	6	&7rt	0.4	24	n/a	n/a	n/a	n/a	n/a	n/a
51	23	4	2	0.7	8	12	9.5	1	2.5	1.6	6.5		0.2	27.5	2.2	12.5	19	L	3	1.2
50	23	4	1	0.7	8	14.5	Bobbin-flyer missing								2.5	19.5	13.5	Circ.	3	1
51	24	5	0	0.7	8	15	8	n/a	n/a	2.4			0.2	29.5						
52	18.5	4	1	1	8	17.7	4.7	3	1.7al	11.6	4.7	—	0.2	34	8	7.5	—	Circ.	3	7.5
53	16	4	0	1.7	6	19	7	3	1.1al	11.3	6	—	0.2	32	9.5	6.5	6.5	Circ.	4	9
54	16.5	4	1	2	8	13	10.5	n/a	n/a	1&1.2	8	4.5rt	0.3	28.5	24	16	4.7	Rect.	3	23.5
55	17	4	0	1.4	12	34	8.5	2	2&2	1.5	13 below	4.5lt	0.5	21	n/a	n/a	n/a	n/a	3	32.5
56	12.5	4	2	1.5	6	14.5	9.5	1	2.5	2.3	10	5lt	n/a	30.5	27	14.5	16.2	Rect.	4	n/a
57	16.7	4	1	1.6	8	16.5	n.a	n.a	n.a	n.a	3.7	4.7rt	0.7	n/a	7	7.5	7.5	Circ.	4	9
99	11.7	Cast	1	0.7	6	13.5	17	n/a	n/a	3.1	16.5		0.6	35.5	29.2	17.5	35.5	Rect.	4	8.7
110	11	4	0	1.7	6	13.7	6.7	n/a	n/a	2	5	—	0.4	23.7	7.2	7.5	—	Circ.	3	8
111	11	1	0	1.2	8	11.5	8.5	1	2.3	1.6	—	—	0.6	20	5.5	7.2	—	Circ.	3	8
112	12	2	1	1.5	6	13	9.5	n/a	n/a	1.8	5.5	—	0.6	21	7	8	8	Circ.	4	8
113	11.2	1	0	1.5	6	13	9.5	n/a	n/a	1.6	5.5	—	0.4	21.5	6.7	7	—	Circ.	3	8
114	14.2	3	2	1.5	6	16.5	8.5	2	2.22	1.2	—	—	0.4	30.7	9.2	7.7	8.5	Heart	3	10
115	12	2	2	1.7	8	14	9.7	1	2.2	2	—	4.5rt	0.2	24	7	8	—	Circ.	4	7

HORIZONTAL BOBBIN-FLYER WHEELS (measurements in inches)

WHEEL NO.	WHEEL Diameter	No. of pieces in rim	Width of rim	No. of grooves in rim	No. of spokes	Height of axle	BOBBIN-FLYER Mother-of-All to wheel axle	Length of bobbin-flyer	No. of grooves in whorl	Diameter of whorl grooves	Diameter of bobbin groove	Size of orifice	Height of orifice	TABLE Length	Width	Slope	LEGS No. of legs	Length of front legs	Length of back legs
29	21	4	2	0	12	23.5	15.5	9	2	1.9	1.5	0.4	26	15.5	6	7.5	3	21	17.7
30	20.5	4	3.25	2	14	30	15	9	1	1.25	0.75	0.5	27.5	17	6.5	4	3	18.2	18.2
31	20	4	3	2	16	31	14.5	9.25	2	1.87/1.75	1.25	0.37	27.5	21.5	6.5	4	3	18.7	17.8
32		3	2	1	8	22.5	21.7	10.7	2	1/1	0.5	0.4	21.5	19.5	5	4.5	3	17	15.5
33	22	6	1.5	0	14	24	16.2	9.25	2	2.1/1.9	1.5	0.4	25	21	4 > 6	3	3	15.5	14.5
34	23.5	1	1.5	1	12	22.7	14.2	10.5	2	1.5/1.6	1.7	0.3	26.5	17.2	5	10	4	20.5	14.5
35	22	4	1.6	1	8	18.5	17.2	9.5	1	2	1.3	0.37	25.2	n/a	n/a	n/a	3	22	22
36	16.5	2	2.75	1	0	20.5	19	8	1	1.5	1.8	0.25	18	25	16 < 8	13.5	3	8	16
37	11(9)	n/a	n/a	1	n/a	13.2	15	5.7	n/a	n/a	0	0.2	12	21.5	4 > 6	0	3	4.2	5.5
59	8.5	1	0.5	2	8	5.5	9.7	5.7	1	1.3	1.1	0.2	5.7	14	7	0	0	0	0
60	20	4	3	1	16	24.5	16	8.5	1	1.75	1.5	0.3	24.5	19	6 > 7	6.7	3	17	13.2
61	20	4	3	0	14	24	15.7	8.5	2	1.5/1.6	1.3	0.3	24.5	18	6	7	3	17.2	13
62	20	4	3	0	16	24	15.5	8.7	2	1.7/1.8	1.1	0.4	25	18	4 > 6	7	3	17	15
63	19	4	2.25	2	12	26	12.7	13	2	1.7/1.8	1.4	0.7	23.5	17.5	6	5.2	3	17.5	14.7
64	21	12	1.7	2	10	20.5	13	8.5	2	2/2	1.4	0.4	26.7	17	4.7	0	4	8.2	8.2
66	22.5	4	1.75	2	12	16	16	10	2	3/3	2.6	0.4	25.7	18	7.2	12.7	4	10.5	10.5
67	23	4	1.75	0	12	18	18.5	9.5	2	2.2/2.1	1.6	0.3	26	17.5	3 > 5	4.2	3	16	14.7
68	26.2	4	2.5	2	12	28.5	21	9.2	2	1.5/1.5	1	0.4	24	19.5	5.2	7	3	17.5	15
69	20.5	4	2.6	2	16	23	14.5	10.2	2	2/1.9	1.3	0.3	25.5	17.3	5.6	5.7	3	14	14
70	19.6	4	2.2	2	12	24	15	8.7	2	1.7/1.5	1.3	0.4	24.5	16	6		3	18	17
72	15.5 / 15.5	4	2	0	8	24	9	8.75 (lower wheel)	2	1.6/1.6	1.1	0.4		n/a	n/a	n/a	4	19	25.5
73	13.5 / 12.5	4	4.4	0	8	22	9	8.5 (lower wheel)	2	1.6/1.6	1			n/a	n/a	n/a	4	19	20.5
74	16	2	2	0	8	26.5	n/a	18.7	n/a	n/a	n/a	0.6	17.5	n/a	n/a	0	4	15.6	15.6
76	30.6 / 40.8	1	n/a	2	0	28.8	10.5	10 (lower wheel)	2	1.6/1.6	1.4	0.4	29.5	14.7	5.7	0	5	9.7	9.7
78	26.2	4	2.2	0	8	29	25	Bobbin-flyer missing					25.5	35	15	0	4	11.5	11.5
79	30.5	1	2	0	12	26.7	27	11.2	1	1.5	1.1	0.5	22.7	29.7	10 < 8	8.7	4	18	13
81	32.7	1	2.3	0	10	26.5	27.2	n/a	1	n/a	1.1	0.4	28.5	29.7	3 > 6	7.8	4	14.5	8.7
82	24.5	4	2.5	2	110	26.5	20.5	9.2	2	1.7/1.7	1.2	0.4		20	5 > 7	5.7	3	19	19

HORIZONTAL BOBBIN-FLYER WHEELS *(measurements in inches)*

WHEEL NO.	WHEEL: Diameter	No. of pieces in rim	Width of rim	No. of grooves in rim	No. of spokes	Height of axle	Mother-of-All to wheel axle	BOBBIN-FLYER: Length of bobbin-flyer	No. of grooves in whorl	Diameter of whorl grooves	Diameter of bobbin groove	Size of orifice	Height of orifice	TABLE: Length	Width	Slope	LEGS: No. of legs	Length of front legs	Length of back legs
83	25.7	4	2.2	2	8	24.5	20	9.7	1	1.5	1	0.4	23.5	22	4.6	7	3	16.5	12.5
84	21	4	3.2	2	12	25.5	15	8.5	2	1.6/1.6	1.2	0.4	25.5	18.2	5 > 8	4.5	3	16.2	16.2
85	17.5	4	2.5	2	14	27.7	14	9.5	2	2.7/2.3	2	0.2	27	17.5	6 > 7	3	3	17.5	16
86	21	4	3.5	2	16	29	15.7	10	2	1.7/1.5	1.2	0.4	27.7	17.5	7 > 8	3.5	3	17.7	16.7
87	26	4	3	2	12	27.2	25	8.5	2	1.4/1.6	0.7	0.25	24.5	21.7	5 > 7	3.2	3	16	16
88	30	4	2.1	2	14	26.5	27	9.5	2	2/1.7	1.5	0.4	26	23.7	4 > 7	5	3	16.5	16.5
89	31	4	2.6	2	12	30.5	23	9.2	2	1.5/1.6	1	0.4	25.5	24	5 > 7	4.5	3	17	16
90	30.5	4	2.1	2	14	30	24.5	9.5	2	1.5/1.5	1	0.4	25.5	23.5	7	4.5	3	19	16.5
91	26	4	2.5	2	12	28.5	21.5	8.25	1	1.5	0.6	0.3	25	20.2	6 > 7	4.2	3	17	17
92	28	4	2.4	1	12	27.2	21.7	9	2	1.5	1	0.4	24	20.7	4 > 6	6	3	16	14.7
93	17.5	4	1.7	2	8	21.5	14.7	9.5	2	1.2/1.2	1.3	0.4	20.2	16	5 > 7	4	3	15	13.7
94	36	4	2.7	2	20	34.5	31	9	2	1.5/1.5	1	0.4	27	32	8 > 9	8.7	3	17.5	13
95	33.7	4	2.7	2	16	30	24.5	10	2	1.7/1.7	1.4	0.4	25.7	28	7 > 8	7.5	3	17	13.5
96	13.7 / 13.7	1	2.5 / 2.1	2	8	27.5 / 19	18.2	9.2	2	1.2/1.2	1.5	0.4	25.5	22.5	7.7	0	4	18.2	18.2
97	16 / 16	1	2.5 / 2.5	1	8	29.5 / 14	18.5	9.5 (lower wheel)	2	1.5/1.4	1.2	0.4	29	23	8.5	0	4	19.5	19.5
98	25.2	4	0.7	2	6	25.7	20	7.5 (lower wheel)	2	1.2/1.4	0.9	0.3	23.5	16	1	6	3	18.7	15.5
99	22	n/a	2.4	1	24-12	25.5	20.5	8	2	1.6/1	1.2	0.75	27.7	21.5	8 > 9	5.2	3	16.5	15.5
116	9	1	1	2	8	33.5	7	6.5	n/a	n/a	0.9	0.2	32.5	9	6	0	4	19 (below 3)	18
117	13	1	1	2	6	17	12	9.5	1	2.5	2	0.3	18	n/a	n/a	n/a	4	18	0.5
118	17.5	4	1.1	0	8	19.5	13	10	1	2.3	2	0.25	20	n/a	n/a	n/a	4	0.5	10
119	13	1	1.9	0	6	17	11	9.5	1	3	1.9	0.4	17	n/a	n/a	n/a	4	16	13
120	13	4	0.7	0	6	11.7	15.5	10.2	2	2.5/2.3	1.7	0.3	23.7	16	4 > 6	9	3	15	13
121	15	1	1.7	2	6	15.2	15	9.7	1	3.8	1.8	0.4	25.7	12.5	5.5	5.2	3	19	13
122	13.2	4	2	2	8,7	14.5	17.5	9.5	1	1.8	1.7	0.4	25	14.2	4 > 5	8	3	15.2	12.5
123	14.5	4	1.5	2	8	17	14.5	8.2	1	2	0.8	0.2	22.5	19.5	4 > 5	4.5	3	17	13
124	18.5	4	1.5	0	8	17.5	21	9.7	1	2.7	1.8	0.4	24.7	18.2	4 > 5	18	3	14.7	9.7
125	15	4	0.9	0	6	13.7	12.5	9	1	2.2	2	0.5	21.2	16.2	4 > 5	5	3	19.2	10.2
126	13.5	1	2.2	2	6	15	17	9.5	1	2.2	2	0.3	27	14.5	5.2	8.7	3	15.2	12.5
127	10.5	1	1.5	2	6	13.5	13	9	1	2.4	1.8	0.4	20.7	11.7	4.7	6.5	3	12	8.7
128	11	4	1.2	2	6	11	10.5	9.5	1	2.5	2	0.5	19	14.2	3 > 5	6.5	3